TRUST
in the
LORD

Publications International, Ltd.

Let's get social!

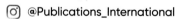 @Publications_International

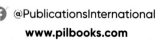 @PublicationsInternational

www.pilbooks.com

Table of Contents

INTRODUCTION

Trust in the Lord with all thine heart;
and lean not unto thine
own understanding. In all thy ways
acknowledge him,
and he shall direct thy paths.

Proverbs 3:5–6

We have many concerns: health, finances, the well-being of our loved ones, and more. It's easy to get bogged down in our daily worries. The more time we spend in prayer, however, the more we learn to trust God. We can turn our concerns over to God in prayer, resting in God's faithful love and knowing that God wants what is best for us.

This devotional contains a collection of Bible verses, prayers, and reflections that focus on trust: trusting in God's wisdom and his plan for us. Ultimately, as we present our desires and petitions to the Lord, we also want to be able to say, as Jesus did, "Thy will be done," trusting that God's plans are the best plans.

'Tis So Sweet to Trust in Jesus

'Tis so sweet to trust in Jesus,
and to take him at his word;
just to rest upon his promise,
and to know,
"Thus saith the Lord."

Jesus, Jesus, how I trust him!
How I've proved him
o'er and o'er!
Jesus, Jesus, precious Jesus!
O for grace to trust him more!

Louisa M. R. Stead

LETTING GO OF WORRIES

∽≈◦≈∽

Casting all your care upon him;
for he careth for you.

1 Peter 5:7

Deliver me out of the mire,
and let me not sink.

Psalm 69:14

No matter the worries I have, small or large, you, O God, are there ahead of me with promises of help and support that relieve me and free me from getting stuck in the mire of my fear. I am grateful.

Know the benediction of
the Lord in these days!

In all your comings and goings,
know he is there. In all your
joys and triumphs, know he
upholds you. In all your worries
and heartaches, know that
he cares.

And in all your worship,
celebrating, dancing, laughing—
wherever you are—know that
he is pleased.

The Lord by wisdom hath founded the earth; by understanding hath he established the heavens. By his knowledge the depths are broken up, and the clouds drop down the dew.

My son, let not them depart from thine eyes: keep sound wisdom and discretion: So shall they be life unto thy soul, and grace to thy neck. Then shalt thou walk in thy way safely, and thy foot shall not stumble. When thou liest down, thou shalt not be afraid: yea, thou shalt lie down, and thy sleep shall be sweet.

Proverbs 3:19–24

Lord, you know the worries that keep me awake some nights. Please deliver me from this fretfulness, and grant me a deep and true trust in you and your wisdom.

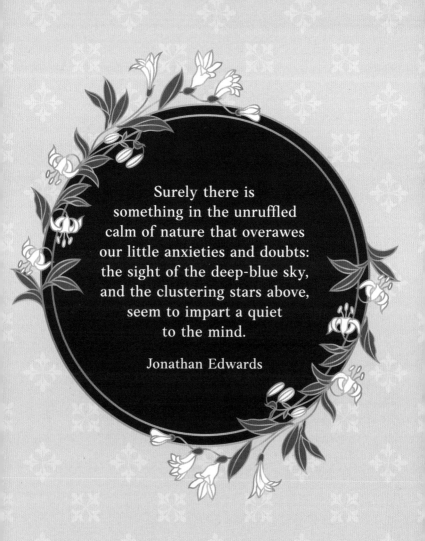

Surely there is
something in the unruffled
calm of nature that overawes
our little anxieties and doubts:
the sight of the deep-blue sky,
and the clustering stars above,
seem to impart a quiet
to the mind.

Jonathan Edwards

> For I the Lord thy God will hold thy
> right hand, saying unto thee, Fear not;
> I will help thee.
>
> Isaiah 41:13

Sometimes, we just need someone to hold our hand. As children, we walked into a strange place and reached for our mother's hand. Her touch calmed us, reducing our uncertainty and fear. Now, when we are alone, or even when we are feeling very grown up, God says he will hold our hand. He will help us. Fear not, he says. He squeezes just a little. And we are calm.

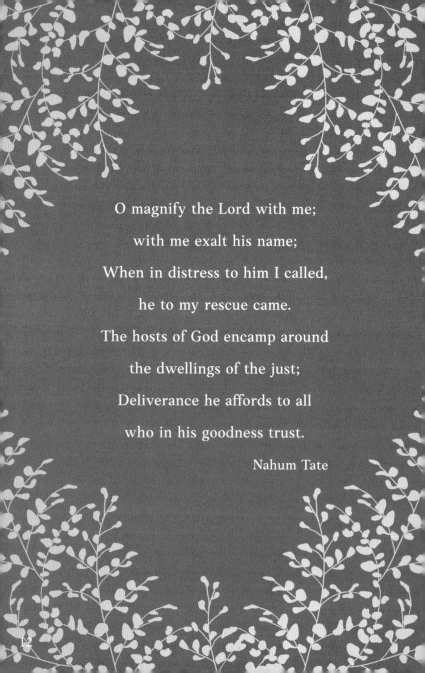

O magnify the Lord with me;

with me exalt his name;

When in distress to him I called,

he to my rescue came.

The hosts of God encamp around

the dwellings of the just;

Deliverance he affords to all

who in his goodness trust.

Nahum Tate

There are many events in our lives over which we have no control. However, we do have a choice either to endure trying times and press on or to give up. The secret of survival, whether or not we question God's presence or his ability to help us, is remembering that our hope is in the fairness, goodness, and justice of God. When we put our trust in the character of a God who cannot fail us, we will remain faithful. Our trust and faithfulness produce the endurance that sees us through the "tough stuff" we all face in this life.

> For I know the thoughts that I think toward you, saith the Lord, thoughts of peace, and not of evil, to give you an expected end.
>
> Jeremiah 29:11

God may throw us a few curve balls in life —we may feel hassled, troubled, anxious, or uncomfortable, and not understand why our circumstances don't fit our desires. But if we trust in the wisdom of his plan, God will provide for all our needs.

He that dwelleth in the secret place of the most High shall abide under the shadow of the Almighty. I will say of the Lord, He is my refuge and my fortress: my God; in him will I trust. Surely he shall deliver thee from the snare of the fowler, and from the noisome pestilence. He shall cover thee with his feathers, and under his wings shalt thou trust: his truth shall be thy shield and buckler.

Psalm 91:1–4

Only when we trust God, do we have peace and assurance in the shelter of his care.

> A friend loveth at all times,
> and a brother is born for adversity.
>
> Proverbs 17:17

When our lives get overloaded, one of the first things we cut back is the time we spend with friends. But it is these very relationships that can center us, ease our stress, and remind us of our true priorities.

But so much the more went there
a fame abroad of him: and great
multitudes came together to hear,
and to be healed by him of
their infirmities. And he withdrew
himself into the wilderness, and prayed.

Luke 5:15–16

When I start to feel overwhelmed by the problems and stresses of everyday life, I know it's time to find a quiet place where I can retreat and rest my mind, body, and spirit. Prayer is good for my soul.

After these things the word of the Lord
came unto Abram in a vision, saying,
Fear not, Abram: I am thy shield,
and thy exceeding great reward.

Genesis 15:1

We respond to stresses in our lives
with either fear or faith. Fear is a great
threat to our faith. That's why we read
often in the scriptures the directive,
"Fear not." The closer we draw to God,
the more our fears diminish.

Fret not thyself because of evildoers, neither be thou envious against the workers of iniquity. For they shall soon be cut down like the grass, and wither as the green herb. Commit thy way unto the Lord; trust also in him; and he shall bring it to pass.

Psalm 37:1–2, 5

Please, Lord, step into this situation. I don't know what to do. Things were done, words were said, and now I'm at odds with someone. Maybe I was wrong, but I don't think so. Honestly, I want to blame the other person for all of it, but maybe I have a blind spot. I want to sort things out and turn things around, but I'm not sure where to start. I don't know if a half-baked apology will do any good, especially if I don't really mean it. And actually, I should be receiving an apology, but I doubt that will ever happen. I beg you, please do your work here. Shine your light so we see things clearly. Use your power to dismantle whatever grudges we have piled up. I commit this whole mess to you.

> For thou art my hope, O Lord God:
> thou art my trust from my youth.
>
> Psalm 71:5

Little children automatically see the good and look for the silver linings. Kids have such hope built into their personalities. I recall when I was young, I had faith and hope that all would be well, even when my parents or family suffered some illness, job loss, or other hardship. I just had that seed of hope in my heart. Now that I am older, I find my hope in God and his presence and love. I still feel that sense of goodness and that all will be well when I am centered in hope and in him. If I keep my heart open, as I did when I was little, and come to God for help, he never fails to give me what I need.

O Lord, thou hast searched me,
and known me. Thou knowest
my downsitting and mine uprising,
thou understandest my thought
afar off. Thou compassest my path
and my lying down, and art
acquainted with all my ways.
For there is not a word in my tongue,
but, lo, O Lord, thou knowest it
altogether.

Psalm 139:1–4

We teach children that the Sun, the Moon, and the stars are always in the sky, even when we cannot see them. Let me trust, Lord, that even when I don't perceive you working in my life, you are still present!

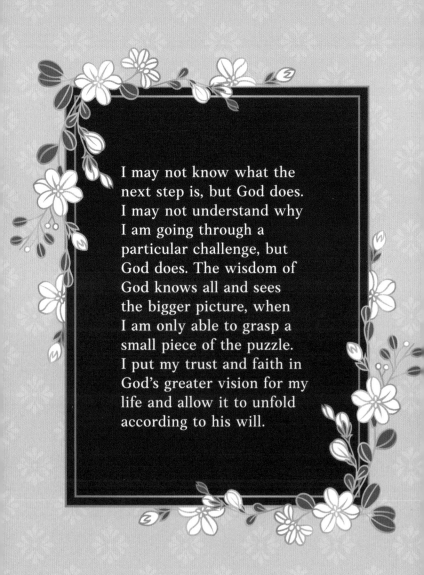

I may not know what the next step is, but God does. I may not understand why I am going through a particular challenge, but God does. The wisdom of God knows all and sees the bigger picture, when I am only able to grasp a small piece of the puzzle. I put my trust and faith in God's greater vision for my life and allow it to unfold according to his will.

My brethren, count it all joy when ye fall into divers temptations; Knowing this, that the trying of your faith worketh patience. But let patience have her perfect work, that ye may be perfect and entire, wanting nothing.

James 1:2–4

As we learn patience, we also learn to trust that God has our best interests in mind.

Wait on the Lord: be of good courage,
and he shall strengthen thine heart:
wait, I say, on the Lord.

Psalm 27:14

Sitting here in this waiting room, O God,
time drags and fear festers. Remake worry
into energized, active prayers, into trust
in the process of healing and recovery.
We're scooting over to make room for you,
a companion for the waiting.

Offer the sacrifices of righteousness,
and put your trust in the Lord.

Psalm 4:5

Dear Lord, my financial demands
exceed the resources I have. The
pressure I feel to do something, even
if it's unwise, is building, and I fear I
will cave in and make a decision I will
regret. Help me trust you. Preserve
my integrity and show me your way
of dealing with this situation.

Be still, and know that I am God.

Psalm 46:10

Dear God, waiting for you is the hardest part of life. Not knowing. Not understanding. Not being able to figure things out. And when you don't provide answers right away, I feel as if I'll go crazy. But when I stop a moment and think about it, it makes sense that there will be times when you ask me to just trust you, when you'll challenge my rhetoric about believing in you and teach me to be patient. So here I am. I'll be still and wait for you.

In the Lord put I my trust:
how say ye to my soul,
Flee as a bird to your mountain?

Psalm 11:1

May I have a moment to speak with you, O God? I know there is so much going on in the world that requires your attention. It's just that sometimes I feel tension getting a grip on me and worry clouds my view. This distances me from you and from everything in my life. I pray for the freedom to worry less. I want to simply trust you more.

> The Lord our God be with us,
> as he was with our fathers: let him
> not leave us, nor forsake us.
>
> 1 Kings 8:57

Lord God, you truly will never leave us or forsake us. You are always near, always watching over us. We will never be alone as long as you are here with us. We do not need to worry or be anxious. We can trust in you. Amen.

Be ye angry, and sin not: let not the sun go down upon your wrath.

Ephesians 4:26

Lord, it's hard to wait for word about my new job. Did I get it? Did they turn me down? I'm so looking forward to starting, so why the delay? Can't they make up their minds?

Yes, I do need patience more than anything else—and right now! Please quell my anger and help me see that if this isn't the right place for me, I can trust you to keep it from me. But it's hard to wait. Still hard to wait.

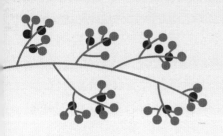

Verily I say unto you, Except ye
be converted, and become as little
children, ye shall not enter into
the kingdom of heaven. Whosoever
therefore shall humble himself
as this little child, the same is greatest
in the kingdom of heaven.

Matthew 18:3–4

When I freeze in worry and indecision, fill
me with the trusting contentment of a child
swinging on a garden gate in arcs of slow, free
motion. Your presence is oil for the hinges.

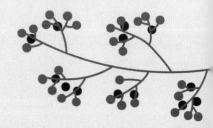

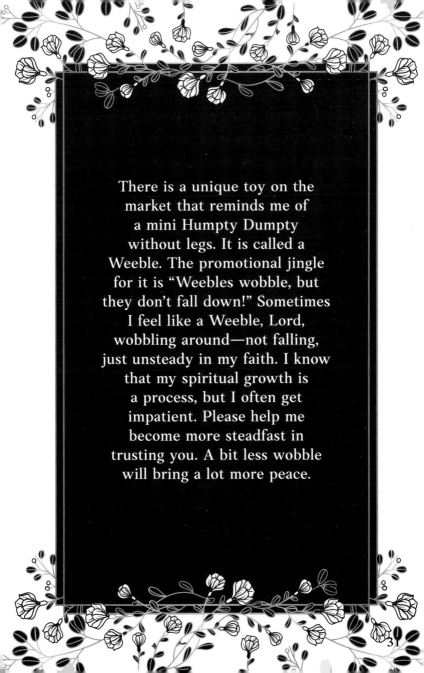

There is a unique toy on the market that reminds me of a mini Humpty Dumpty without legs. It is called a Weeble. The promotional jingle for it is "Weebles wobble, but they don't fall down!" Sometimes I feel like a Weeble, Lord, wobbling around—not falling, just unsteady in my faith. I know that my spiritual growth is a process, but I often get impatient. Please help me become more steadfast in trusting you. A bit less wobble will bring a lot more peace.

With men this is impossible; but with
God all things are possible.

Matthew 19:26

All things are possible to those who
have faith. Putting our trust in God
gives us wings to soar higher, dream
bigger, and go farther than we thought
we ever could. We rest in faith, like
a comfortable chair, relaxed in the
knowing that whatever we need will
be given to us in God's due time. What
a wonderful feeling, to have an
unshakeable faith and an immovable
trust in his will for us!

It is better to trust in the Lord than
to put confidence in man.

Psalm 118:8

When we struggle in unfamiliar territory,
Lord, we feel your calming, guiding hand and
remember that you have always been faithful
to your children. Then we know that our
journey is safe. Please continue to give us
confidence as we move to where you are
calling us.

> He maketh the storm a calm,
> so that the waves thereof are still.
>
> Psalm 107:29

Calm me enough, O Lord, to breathe
deeply and restoratively. Prayer restores
me in the presence of all that threatens
to undo me, which I name to you now.

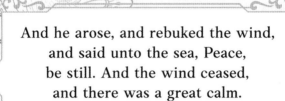

And he arose, and rebuked the wind,
and said unto the sea, Peace,
be still. And the wind ceased,
and there was a great calm.

Mark 4:39

Show me a sign, dear God, to help me
figure out this problem I am struggling
with. Give me something my spirit will
recognize to help me overcome what
stands in the way of my happiness. Help
me, God, to see your solution as the calm
within the storm.

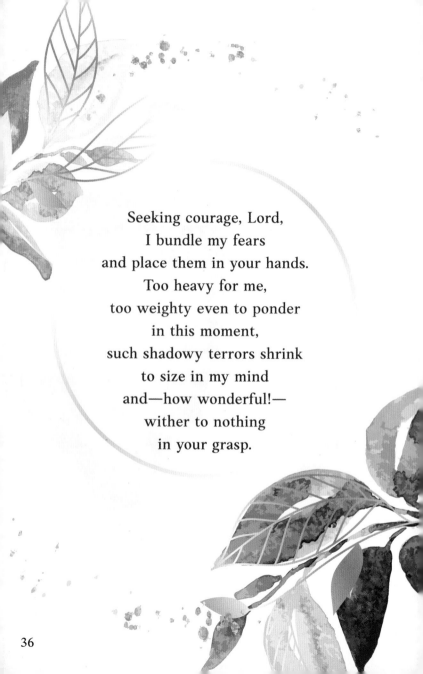

Seeking courage, Lord,
I bundle my fears
and place them in your hands.
Too heavy for me,
too weighty even to ponder
in this moment,
such shadowy terrors shrink
to size in my mind
and—how wonderful!—
wither to nothing
in your grasp.

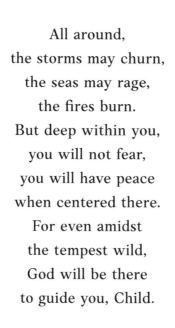

All around,
the storms may churn,
the seas may rage,
the fires burn.
But deep within you,
you will not fear,
you will have peace
when centered there.
For even amidst
the tempest wild,
God will be there
to guide you, Child.

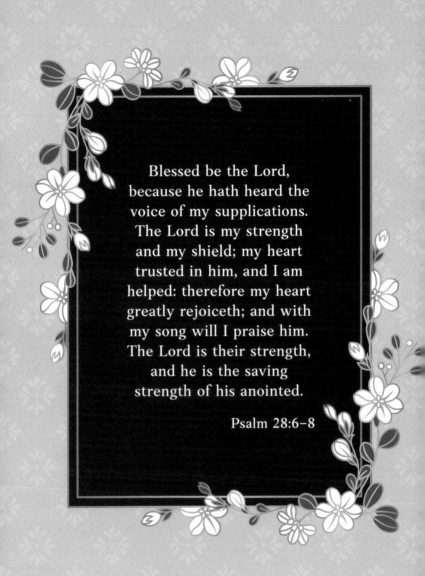

Blessed be the Lord,
because he hath heard the
voice of my supplications.
The Lord is my strength
and my shield; my heart
trusted in him, and I am
helped: therefore my heart
greatly rejoiceth; and with
my song will I praise him.
The Lord is their strength,
and he is the saving
strength of his anointed.

Psalm 28:6–8

And ye shall serve the Lord your God,
and he shall bless thy bread,
and thy water; and I will take
sickness away from the midst of thee.

Exodus 23:25

Help me recover from this ambush of illness,
Great Physician, and the worry it brings.
Reassure my fearful heart that my sickness
was never intended; it just happened. Bodies
break down, parts age, and minds weary. Your
assurance gives me strength to hang on.

> The Lord is my light
> and my salvation; whom shall I fear?
> the Lord is the strength of my life;
> of whom shall I be afraid?
>
> Psalm 27:1

In the midst of the darkness that threatens to overwhelm us lies a pinpoint of light, a persistent flicker that guides us through the pain and fear, through the hopelessness and despair, to a place of peace and healing on the other side. This is God's Spirit, leading us back home like the lighthouse beacon that directs the ships through the fog to the safety of the harbor.

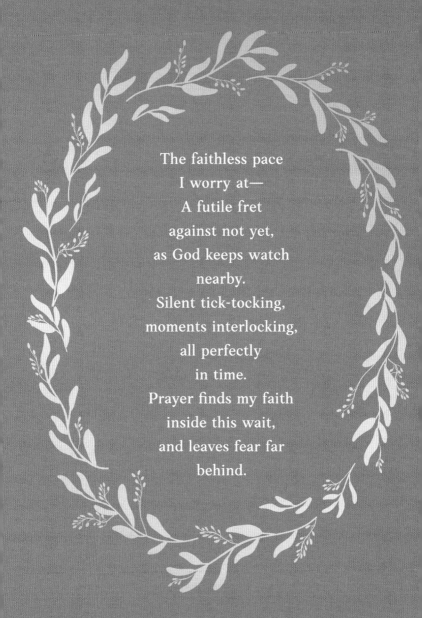

The faithless pace
I worry at—
A futile fret
against not yet,
as God keeps watch
nearby.
Silent tick-tocking,
moments interlocking,
all perfectly
in time.
Prayer finds my faith
inside this wait,
and leaves fear far
behind.

Are not five sparrows sold
for two farthings, and not one of
them is forgotten before God?
But even the very hairs of your
head are all numbered.
Fear not therefore: ye are of more
value than many sparrows.

Luke 12:6–7

Spirit, help me live one day at a
time so that I may meet each day's
challenges with grace, courage, and
hope. Shelter me from the fears
of the future and the anguish of
the past. Keep my mind and heart
focused on the present, where the
true gift of happiness and healing is
to be found. Amen.

Therefore, my beloved brethren,
be ye stedfast, unmoveable,
always abounding in the work of
the Lord, forasmuch as ye know that
your labour is not in vain in the Lord.

1 Corinthians 15:58

It's amazing, steadfast God, how much
better I feel after sharing with you even
the smallest doubt or little niggling
worry about being the best parent I can
be. Connected, we can do great things.
Alone, I am the victim of my own fears.

In God I will praise his word, in God
I have put my trust; I will not fear
what flesh can do unto me.

Psalm 56:4

Lord, I wish to live a long life, but I
fear growing old. I want to accomplish
great things, but I fear risking what I
already have. I desire to love with all
my heart, but the prospect of self-
revelation makes me shrink back.
Perhaps for just this day, you would
help me reach out? Let me bypass
these dreads and see instead your hand
reaching back to mine—right now—
just as it always has.

A merry heart maketh a cheerful countenance:
but by sorrow of the heart the spirit is broken.

Proverbs 15:13

Thank you for the funny bone, Lord, placed
next to hearts broken by anxiety and fear. A
good belly laugh is a gift from you, expanding
and healing heart, lungs, and mind.

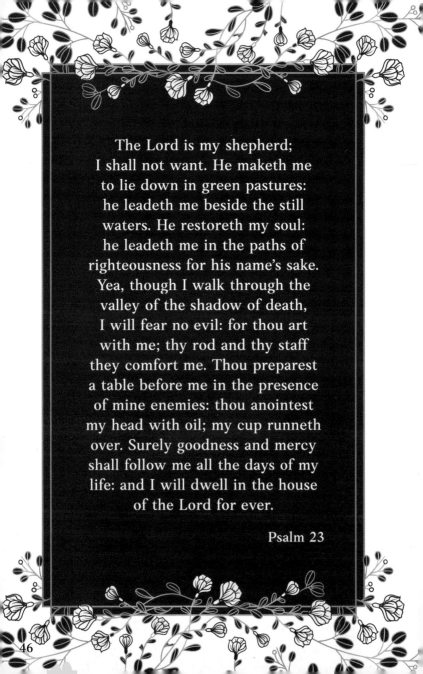

The Lord is my shepherd;
I shall not want. He maketh me
to lie down in green pastures:
he leadeth me beside the still
waters. He restoreth my soul:
he leadeth me in the paths of
righteousness for his name's sake.
Yea, though I walk through the
valley of the shadow of death,
I will fear no evil: for thou art
with me; thy rod and thy staff
they comfort me. Thou preparest
a table before me in the presence
of mine enemies: thou anointest
my head with oil; my cup runneth
over. Surely goodness and mercy
shall follow me all the days of my
life: and I will dwell in the house
of the Lord for ever.

Psalm 23

Within the valleys of mountainous terrain, darkness lingers long in the morning and swoops down to settle swiftly in the evening. The taller the surrounding mountaintops, the deeper and darker the valley. The psalm writer has one of these deep valleys in mind—a place where the path is shadowy and a chill is always in the air.

Yet here, in what some might call a godforsaken place, the psalm writer surprises us with these words: "I will fear no evil: for thou art with me." He surprises and comforts us with his reminder that when we follow the Lord our shepherd, there is no such thing as a godforsaken place.

Dear Lord,

Teach my children to follow my lead
in actions and deeds and to model my
behavior more so than my words. Often
I speak in frustration, but I always act
in patience, kindness, and love. I want
the same for my children. Help them do
as I do, not as I say. Help my spouse see
beyond my occasional sharp or impatient
words, my words of confusion, fear, and
annoyance when things aren't going the
way I would like. Help my family to see
the love I give, the work I do, the way I
live and move and have my being. Amen.

Blessed is the man that trusteth in
the Lord, and whose hope the Lord is.

Jeremiah 17:7

Lord, help me remember that you are the
God of hope. You don't want me to feel sad
or hopeless. It isn't your plan for me to live in
fear or doubt. Help me to feel and access the
power of the Holy Spirit. I know that through
your Spirit I will find the hope and joy and
peace you have promised to your people.

Be strong and of a good courage, fear not, nor be afraid of them: for the Lord thy God, he it is that doth go with thee; he will not fail thee, nor forsake thee.

Deuteronomy 31:6

Dear Lord,

I ask in prayer today for courage and strength to face some big challenges before me. I admit I am anxious, and even afraid, but I know in my heart you will never give me anything I cannot handle, and that you will be by my side the whole way. Instill in me a strong heart and spirit as I deal with my problems and keep my mind centered and focused on the solutions you set before me. I ask nothing more than your presence alongside me as I overcome these obstacles and learn the lessons each one has for my life. I thank you, Lord, for always being there for me in my times of need and struggle. Amen.

Fear none of those things which thou shalt suffer: behold, the devil shall cast some of you into prison, that ye may be tried; and ye shall have tribulation ten days: be thou faithful unto death, and I will give thee a crown of life.

Revelation 2:10

Dear Lord,

I pray for a strong spirit to stand against my fears today. I don't ask for fearlessness, because I do feel fear, and I do worry and doubt and I am human. Instead, I pray that you will be at my side in frightening situations, and that you will never leave me abandoned and forgotten. I pray you will shore up my own spirit and give me a sharp mind and deep faith, so that I can overcome any blocks in the road to love, peace and happiness. Lord, stand beside me, and hold my hand, but also give me that extra bit of courage for the times you ask that I walk through the darkness alone. Thank you, Lord. Amen.

Faith is a key that
opens the door of
abundance. Too many of us
live behind locked doors of lack,
suffering and loneliness when
everything we could possibly desire
is on the other side, if only we turn
the key. God has promised us
abundant blessings, but first we must
show him we have faith by moving
towards the door without doubt,
fear and uncertainty. Then, he
will reveal a bounty of
blessings to reward us.

> These things I have spoken unto you,
> that in me ye might have peace.
>
> John 16:33

Surrender to the peacefulness of a day spent knowing you did your best. That is all God asks of you, that you offer your best and leave the rest to him. Knowing this, you can relax and not spend wasted time worrying about regrets of the past or concerns of the future, because each moment spent in alignment with God's will takes care of itself.

TRUST AT ALL TIMES

Trust in him at all times;
ye people, pour out your heart
before him:
God is a refuge for us.

Psalm 62:8

O keep my soul, and deliver me:
  let me not be ashamed;
  for I put my trust in thee.

Psalm 25:20

Whatever each day brings, at the end of it,
I kneel silently in your presence; bow my
heart to your wisdom; lift my hands for your
mercy. And open my soul to the great gift:
I am already held in your arms.

And the people, when they knew it,
followed him: and he received them,
and spake unto them of
the kingdom of God, and healed them
that had need of healing.

Luke 9:11

We don't really know why we have to get
sick, Lord. We only know your promise: No
matter where we are or what we are called
to endure, there you are in the midst of it
with us, never leaving our side. Not for a
split second. Thank you, Lord of all.

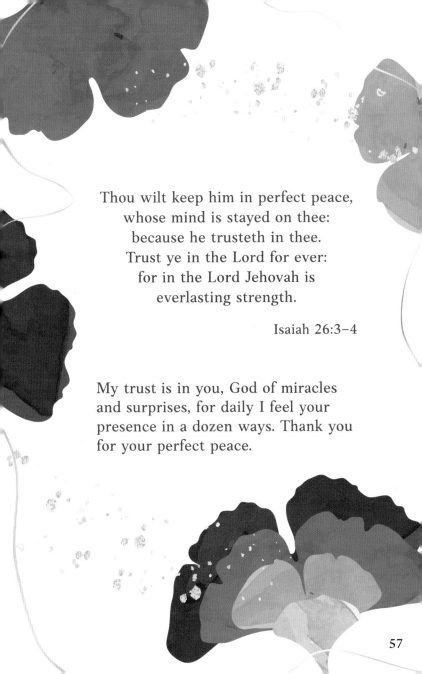

Thou wilt keep him in perfect peace,
whose mind is stayed on thee:
because he trusteth in thee.
Trust ye in the Lord for ever:
for in the Lord Jehovah is
everlasting strength.

Isaiah 26:3–4

My trust is in you, God of miracles
and surprises, for daily I feel your
presence in a dozen ways. Thank you
for your perfect peace.

Then came Peter to him, and said,
Lord, how oft shall my brother sin
against me, and I forgive him?
till seven times? Jesus saith unto him,
I say not unto thee, Until seven times:
but, Until seventy times seven.

Matthew 18:21–22

God, we know that pain has produced
some wisdom in our lives, but it has also
created cynicism and fear. People turn on
us, reject us, hurt us, and none of us wants
to play the fool more than once, so we're
tempted to close off our hearts to people
and to you. But relationships that bring
meaning and joy require vulnerability. Help
us trust you to be our truest friend and to
lead us to the kind of community that will
bring healing rather than destruction.

The Lord will strengthen him upon the bed of languishing: thou wilt make all his bed in his sickness.

Psalm 41:3

When illness strikes, the effects go beyond the physical suffering. Fear, despair, and terrible isolation arise as the illness prolongs itself. It feels natural to lash out at your failing body, medicine that does not help, and even at the God who allowed this terrible thing to happen to you. The fate of the patient's loved ones can be equally painful, as they stand by feeling helpless to be of any real assistance. Yet, be assured that the Lord is there among you.

Thou visitest the earth, and waterest
it: thou greatly enrichest it with the
river of God, which is full of water:
thou preparest them corn, when thou
hast so provided for it.

Psalm 65:9

One of the Hebrew names for God is Jehovah
Jireh (JY-rah). Besides having a nice ring to
it, its meaning—"God, our provider"—is
one worth remembering. In life, we may
experience times of abundance and also
times when we struggle to make ends meet.
In any situation, God asks us to trust and
honor him as Jehovah Jireh, the God who
provides all that we truly need.

Now the Lord of peace himself
give you peace always by all means.
The Lord be with you all.

2 Thessalonians 3:16

Oh Lord, when I see terrible, fearful
events—explosions destroying whole
buildings, droughts that turn crops to
dust, storms devastating all in their
path—then I turn to you. And you are
always here, listening, caring, and
waiting for all of us to reach out to
you. Amen.

They prevented me in the day of my calamity: but the Lord was my stay. He brought me forth also into a large place; he delivered me, because he delighted in me.

Psalm 18:18–19

~~~

So many terrors and troubles confronts us, so many dangers and calamities. Is anyone ever completely safe? Only when we trust God, do we know peace and assurance in the shelter of his care.

And Jesus answering saith unto them, Have faith in God. For verily I say unto you, That whosoever shall say unto this mountain, Be thou removed, and be thou cast into the sea; and shall not doubt in his heart, but shall believe that those things which he saith shall come to pass; he shall have whatsoever he saith. Therefore I say unto you, What things soever ye desire, when ye pray, believe that ye receive them, and ye shall have them.

Mark 11:22–24

Lord, help me trust you enough to tear down the walls of fear and doubt.

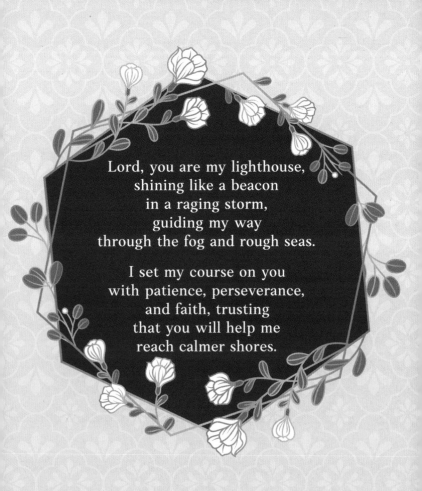

Lord, you are my lighthouse,
shining like a beacon
in a raging storm,
guiding my way
through the fog and rough seas.

I set my course on you
with patience, perseverance,
and faith, trusting
that you will help me
reach calmer shores.

It is of the Lord's mercies that
we are not consumed,
because his compassions fail not.
They are new every morning: great
is thy faithfulness. The Lord is my
portion, saith my soul; therefore will
I hope in him. The Lord is good unto
them that wait for him, to the soul
that seeketh him. It is good that
a man should both hope and quietly
wait for the salvation of the Lord.

Lamentations 3:22–26

Lord, give us hope. Please help us to put
our trust in you. Amen.

For he shall give his angels charge
over thee, to keep thee
in all thy ways.

Psalm 91:11

Father God, teach me to trust your
protection. It's so hard sometimes to find
my way home. The nights get dark. The
clouds hide the stars. If I could learn to
hold the hand of your angels, I know you
would lead me all the way.

But the wisdom that is from
above is first pure, then
peaceable, gentle, and easy
to be intreated, full of mercy
and good fruits, without partiality,
and without hypocrisy.

James 3:17

It's late at night, and still there is much
to do. Yet there is peace, holding onto
childlike trust that God is an
ever-present companion,
showing us how not to
worry needlessly,
burning the candle
at both ends.

Lord, you made me. You can fix me.
You put these corpuscles together.
You knitted my nerves.
You wrote my DNA.
You taught me how to laugh
and how to love.
Something's wrong now,
the system's crashing.
I trust you to make it better.
But what does "better" mean?
Healthy, yes, but whole again.
Body, mind, feelings in balance,
relationships in sync,
My spirit soaring with yours.
Lord, you created me and called
your creation good.
Make me whole again.
Amen.

Lo, children are an heritage of
the Lord: and the fruit of
the womb is his reward.

Psalm 127:3

Whenever I worry that I don't know what I'm
doing as a parent, I remind myself that God
trusted me enough to make me one. His belief
in me renews my belief in myself.

> Then spake Jesus again
> unto them, saying, I am the light of
> the world: he that followeth me
> shall not walk in darkness,
> but shall have the light of life.
>
> John 8:12

You have made things problematic again, Lord, and I need to see that all this upheaval can be a good thing. Help me, Lord. And thank you for showing me that a thoroughly comfortable existence can rob me of real life.

In this time of great change, help me, God of tomorrow, tomorrow, and tomorrow, to trust your guiding presence. Inspire me to follow in the footsteps of ancient desert nomads who wore tiny lanterns on their shoes to give just enough light for the next step. All I really need.

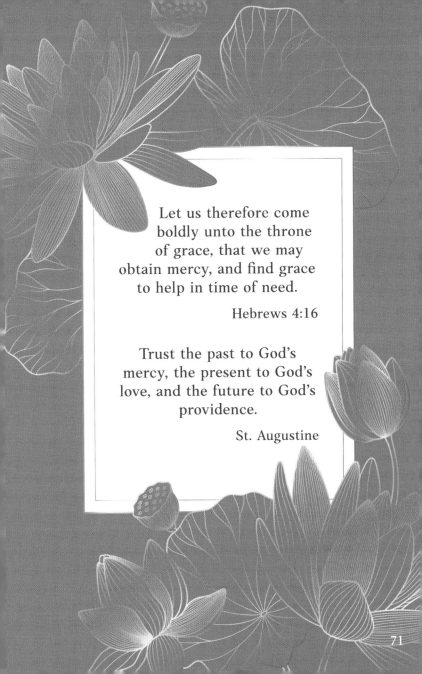

Let us therefore come
boldly unto the throne
of grace, that we may
obtain mercy, and find grace
to help in time of need.

Hebrews 4:16

Trust the past to God's
mercy, the present to God's
love, and the future to God's
providence.

St. Augustine

For by grace are ye saved through faith;
and that not of yourselves: it is the gift
of God: Not of works,
lest any man should boast.

Ephesians 2:8–9

Every day I blow it. Every day I need your
grace, Lord. I am thankful that it isn't
necessary to live a perfect life to have access
to your grace. If that were the case, I'd be in
big trouble. But instead of turning your back
on me when I veer from your paths, you are
always ready to welcome me with open arms.
You simply call me to trust in your saving,
relationship-restoring grace. That's where I'm
standing right now—in that amazing grace of
yours, asking you to forgive and restore me
once again so I can resume good fellowship
with you.

The God of my rock; in him will
I trust: he is my shield, and the horn
of my salvation, my high tower,
and my refuge, my savior.

2 Samuel 22:3

When the winds of change and challenge blow
hard into my life, I will take refuge in you, O
Lord. When the darkness descends upon my
house and home, I will fear not for I will place
my faith in you, O Lord. When my child is ill
or my spouse is hurt, I will remain steadfast,
for I know that you will be right there by my
side, O Lord. Although I cannot see you, I
know you are always with me, O Lord, and in
that I take comfort and find strength.

Dear Lord,

I ask in prayer today for courage and strength to face some big challenges before me. I admit I am anxious, and even afraid, but I know in my heart you will never give me anything I cannot handle, and that you will be by my side the whole way. Instill in me a strong heart and spirit as I deal with my problems and keep my mind centered and focused on the solutions you set before me. I ask nothing more than your presence alongside me as I overcome these obstacles and learn the lessons each one has for my life. I thank you, Lord, for always being there for me in my times of need and struggle. Amen.

> Be of good courage, and let us play
> the men for our people, and for the
> cities of our God: and the Lord do
> that which seemeth him good.
>
> 2 Samuel 10:12

God,

There are times when I act small in the world because I'm afraid to get out of my comfort zone. I'm scared of looking foolish, or failing terribly and letting people down. Yet, you've given me talents and abilities and I long to use them for good in the world. Help me, God, to find that courageous lion within me, and to go forward with trust and inner strength, knowing that whatever comes up, you'll help me through it. I pray for your will to be done in my life, and for the fearlessness that comes from having you as my rock and my foundation. Let me shine my light, God, and help me not play it safe and miss out on the incredible experiences you have in store for me. Amen.

> The fear of man bringeth a snare:
> but whoso putteth his trust
> in the Lord shall be safe.
>
> Proverbs 29:25

Dear Lord,

Thank you for the courage you've given me
to pursue my dreams. So many of my friends
have settled for lives filled with regrets and
unfulfilled dreams, and I've been so blessed
by you with the inner fire and drive to take
my divinely-given talents and do something
with them. No matter how hard I worked,
I knew that I could not achieve such goals
without you and I've always strived to keep
your presence close at hand in all my
decisions and choices. Thank you, Lord, for
helping me find that extra strength within to
face my fears, my doubts and my insecurities
and go for a life well-lived. Amen.

But none of these things
move me, neither count
I my life dear unto myself,
so that I might finish my course
with joy, and the ministry,
which I have received of
the Lord Jesus, to testify
the gospel of the grace of God.

Acts 20:24

God, it's hard to hold the course
when so many obstacles are
thrown in my way. I ask your
help navigating through my
days with a powerful faith and a
steadfast trust that I can do this
thing called life, and do it with
grace and joy. Please help me
stay the course!

> But the Comforter, which is
> the Holy Ghost, whom the Father will
> send in my name, he shall teach you
> all things, and bring all things to
> your remembrance, whatsoever
> I have said unto you.
>
> John 14:26

Holy Spirit, thank you for all that you have taught me. I am grateful for those times when I have been able to sense your presence, when you have led me to discern the Father's will. And I am grateful for those times when you seemed absent, but looking back, I can see you at work. Please help me trust in your wisdom always and at all times.

Almighty God who seest that
we have no power of ourselves
to help ourselves; keep us both
outwardly in our bodies,
and inwardly in our souls;
that we may be defended
from all adversities which may
happen to the body, and from
all evil thoughts which may
assault and hurt the soul;
through Jesus Christ our Lord.
Amen.

6th-century prayer

Friendships end, and it can really hurt when someone decides they don't want to be a part of our lives anymore. We feel rejected, guilty, and broken. Truth is, people who don't want to be in our lives weren't meant to stay. This is when we must turn to God in faith and understand that his plan for us may not include the people we think it should. God knows best whom we have outgrown. So when a friendship reaches the final bend in the road, trust that God is going to lead us around the corner to something —and someone—new. Be assured God knows who we should walk our path with, and when to let go and walk alone.

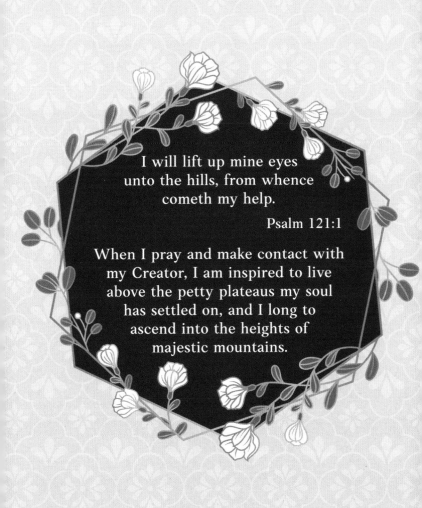

I will lift up mine eyes
unto the hills, from whence
cometh my help.

Psalm 121:1

When I pray and make contact with
my Creator, I am inspired to live
above the petty plateaus my soul
has settled on, and I long to
ascend into the heights of
majestic mountains.

Every word of God is pure:
he is a shield unto them
that put their trust in him.

Proverbs 30:5

It's hard, Lord, to reveal my heart to you, though it's the thing I most want to do. Remind me in this dialogue that you already know what is within me. You wait—thank you!—hoping for the gift of my willingness to acknowledge the good you already see and the bad you've long forgotten. Let me trust fully in your grace.

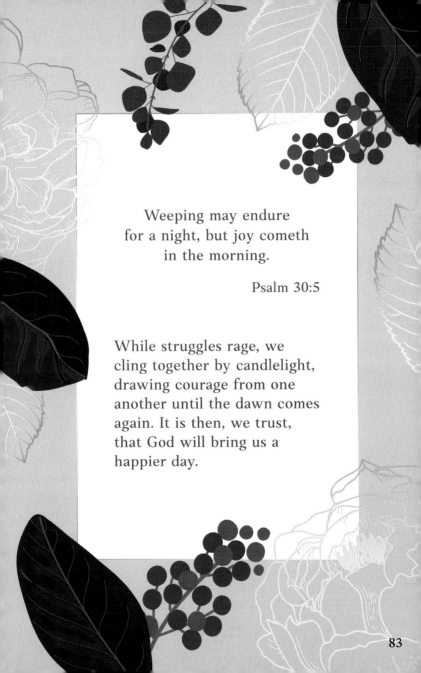

Weeping may endure
for a night, but joy cometh
in the morning.

Psalm 30:5

While struggles rage, we
cling together by candlelight,
drawing courage from one
another until the dawn comes
again. It is then, we trust,
that God will bring us a
happier day.

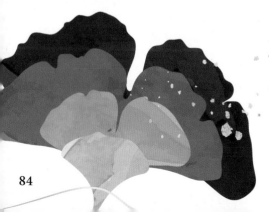

Thou art my hiding place;
thou shalt preserve me from trouble;
thou shalt compass me about
with songs of deliverance.

Psalm 32:7

Lord, my heart was broken, but I
know you can fix it. As I learn to
depend on you, give me the same
thing you gave your servant David:
strength and a song. Amen.

For all things are for your sakes,
that the abundant grace might
through the thanksgiving of
many redound to the glory of God.
For which cause we faint not;
but though our outward man perish,
yet the inward man is renewed
day by day.

2 Corinthians 4:15–16

My Creator, blessed is your presence. For you and you alone give me power to walk through dark valleys into the light again. You and you alone give me hope when there seems no end to my suffering. You and you alone give me peace when the noise of my life overwhelms me. I ask that you give this same power, hope, and peace to all who know discouragement, that they, too, may be emboldened and renewed by your everlasting love. Amen.

The Lord is good,
a strong hold
in the day of trouble;
and he knoweth them
that trust in him.

Nahum 1:7

Lord, for the mercies of this night
My humble thanks I pay
And unto thee I give myself
Today and every day. Amen.

Traditional prayer

> Behold, God is my salvation; I will trust, and not be afraid: for the Lord Jehovah is my strength and my song; he also is become my salvation.
>
> Isaiah 12:2

Dear God, your love embraces me like the warmth of the sun, and I am filled with light. Your hope enfolds me in arms so strong, I lack for nothing. Your grace fills me with the strength I need to move through this day. For these gifts you give me, of eternal love, eternal peace, and most of all, for eternal friendship, I thank you God.

Sometimes I'm like Peter,
and I walk on water.
I stand above my circumstances,
which are like the swirling
tempests of the sea.
But then, like Peter,
I take my eyes off Jesus
and concentrate
on things below.
Soon I start to sink.
How I long to have
a consistent
water-walking
eyes-on-Jesus
faith.

O Lord my God, in thee do
I put my trust: save me from all them
that persecute me, and deliver me.

Psalm 7:1

No one likes suffering. But it brings our
attention back to God and reminds us
how helpless we are without him.

And even to your old age I am he;
and even to hoar hairs will
I carry you: I have made,
and I will bear; even I will carry,
and will deliver you.

Isaiah 46:4

Growing older doesn't necessitate letting go of faith. Even though our bodies are getting older and our thinking may not be as sharp as it once was, God is still the same. We can always depend on him.

To every thing there is a season,
and a time to every purpose
under the heaven.

Ecclesiastes 3:1

Throughout life, patience is the virtue
many people find most difficult to attain
and practice. The seasonal workings of
nature can provide the
perfect inspiration.

Rejoice when I run into problems? Know trials are good for me? Things like that aren't easy—learning to trust patiently.

Growing in grace is a process. Developing character hurts. Becoming more Christ-like in all things is an everyday process called work.

But I have faith it is possible, faith knowing God loves and cares, that all my burdens and trials he also feels and shares.

And when he had called unto him his twelve disciples, he gave them power against unclean spirits, to cast them out, and to heal all manner of sickness and all manner of disease.

Matthew 10:1

Dear Father, thy child is sick.
Look upon me in tender mercy,
and if it be thy will, raise me up
and grant me health and strength.
Amen.

Traditional prayer

The law of truth was in his mouth,
and iniquity was not found
in his lips: he walked with me
in peace and equity, and did turn
many away from iniquity.

Malachi 2:6

Sometimes we believe our souls can only be at peace if there is no outer turmoil. The wonder of God's peace is that even when the world around us is in confusion and our emotions are in a whirl, underneath it all we can know his peace.

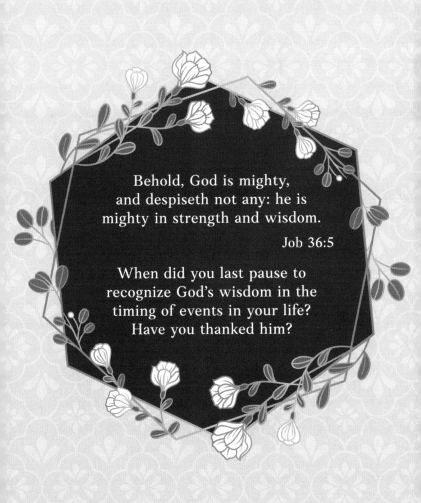

Behold, God is mighty,
and despiseth not any: he is
mighty in strength and wisdom.

Job 36:5

When did you last pause to
recognize God's wisdom in the
timing of events in your life?
Have you thanked him?

Thus saith the Lord, In an acceptable time have I heard thee, and in a day of salvation have I helped thee.

Isaiah 49:8

Keep us from being ruled by time, Lord. You always create time and space for anything we are doing that brings you glory. Teach us to rest in the knowledge that time is in your hands. Whenever we think we don't have enough of it, show us you have plenty and are happy to share! Thank you, Lord, for your generous supply of time.

But we had the sentence of death
in ourselves, that we should not trust
in ourselves, but in God which raiseth
the dead: Who delivered us from
so great a death, and doth deliver:
in whom we trust that
he will yet deliver us.

2 Corinthians 1:9–10

Lord, once again I am aware that you, by your grace, gave me the strength to work through a situation that I was woefully unprepared to face. I accept that when we are completely out of ideas, drained of all energy, and so sick at heart we can barely breathe, your grace and strength lift us up and carry us forward. Thank you, Lord.

Seek not ye what ye shall eat,
or what ye shall drink,
neither be ye of doubtful mind.

Luke 12:29

Lord, this healing process is sometimes
slow, and I get discouraged and filled with
doubt. Can I take this? Will I make it? Yet
you always remind me of your powerful
presence and assure me that where I am
unable to go, you will go for me and what
I am unable to do by myself, you will do
for me. Thank you, Lord. Amen.

> When I consider thy heavens,
> the work of thy fingers, the moon
> and the stars, which thou hast
> ordained; What is man,
> that thou art mindful of him?
>
> Psalm 8:3–4

Lord, with each breath I take I am aware that it is you who breathed life into me. My next breath is as dependent on you as my last breath was. And I can confidently trust in the knowledge that it will be you and you alone who will determine when the last breath leaves my body and I go to be with you. Today, Lord, I thank you for the gift of life and for each breath I take.

PRAYERS FOR OTHERS

For this cause I bow my knees unto the
Father of our Lord Jesus Christ, Of whom
the whole family in heaven and earth is
named, That he would grant you, according
to the riches of his glory, to be strengthened
with might by his Spirit in the inner man;
That Christ may dwell in your hearts by
faith; that ye, being rooted and grounded in
love, May be able to comprehend with all
saints what is the breadth, and length, and
depth, and height; And to know the love of
Christ, which passeth knowledge, that ye
might be filled with all the fulness of God.

Ephesians 3:14–19

Jesus said unto him, Thou shalt love
the Lord thy God with all thy heart,
and with all thy soul,
and with all thy mind. This is the first
and great commandment.
And the second is like unto it, Thou
shalt love thy neighbour as thyself.
On these two commandments hang all
the law and the prophets.

Matthew 22:37–40

We trust in the Lord to care for us, and he,
in turn, trusts in us to care for each other.
We can honor his faith in us by pledging to
serve our communities. We can truly live
his love by caring for our neighbors.

> For where two or three are gathered
> together in my name,
> there am I in the midst of them.
>
> Matthew 18:20

Lord, I often pray for others when I need
to pray with others. Show me the power of
shared prayer as I meet with others in your
name and in your presence. I place my trust
in you to guide me to faithful prayer partners.
Amen.

Awake, O north wind; and come, thou south; blow upon my garden, that the spices thereof may flow out. Let my beloved come into his garden, and eat his pleasant fruits.

Song of Solomon 4:16

Marriage, Lord, is like a garden: You don't keep digging up a plant to see if its roots are growing! Sustain us, for there are seasons of wilted growth just as there are seasons of blossom and fruit. While ripening to become useful, may we love one another with the same strengthening trust and patience you, gardener of the world, show toward us.

And the Lord went before them
by day in a pillar of a cloud, to lead
them the way; and by night in a pillar
of fire, to give them light; to go
by day and night.

Exodus 13:21

As my husband and children go out into the
world, it is comforting to know that the Lord
goes before them to lead the way and to give
them light. It's hard sometimes, but I trust
the wisdom of God's plan for them.

Charity suffereth long, and is kind;
charity envieth not; charity vaunteth
not itself, is not puffed up,
Doth not behave itself unseemly,
seeketh not her own, is not
easily provoked, thinketh no evil;
Rejoiceth not in iniquity, but rejoiceth
in the truth; Beareth all things,
believeth all things, hopeth all things,
endureth all things.

1 Corinthians 13:4–7

Thank you, Lord, for our marriage.
Like a wedding band, our love encircles
but doesn't bind. Like a vow, our love
is words but sustains because of what
they mean. In your grace, our love has
the permanence of rock, not of walls,
but of a bridge to moments ahead as
special and bright as when we first met.

He that trusteth in his
own heart is a fool:
but whoso walketh
wisely, he shall
be delivered.

Proverbs 28:26

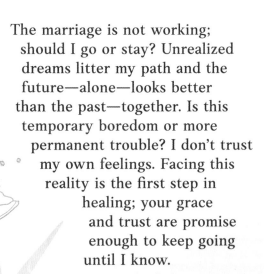

The marriage is not working;
should I go or stay? Unrealized
dreams litter my path and the
future—alone—looks better
than the past—together. Is this
temporary boredom or more
permanent trouble? I don't trust
my own feelings. Facing this
reality is the first step in
healing; your grace
and trust are promise
enough to keep going
until I know.

And they shall teach no more every
man his neighbour, and every man
his brother, saying, Know the Lord:
for they shall all know me,
from the least of them unto
the greatest of them, saith the Lord:
for I will forgive their iniquity, and I
will remember their sin no more.

Jeremiah 31:34

I never meant to be a failure, Lord, never
meant to break commitments. But I am and
I did. Comfort me, for I mourn the loss of
innocence that crumbled beneath the
knowledge that I couldn't stay in the
marriage and be okay. Forgive my failures;
heal my regrets and fortify my courage.
Help me grieve and go on free from toxic,
wasteful hate. And as I do, help me forgive
those left behind.

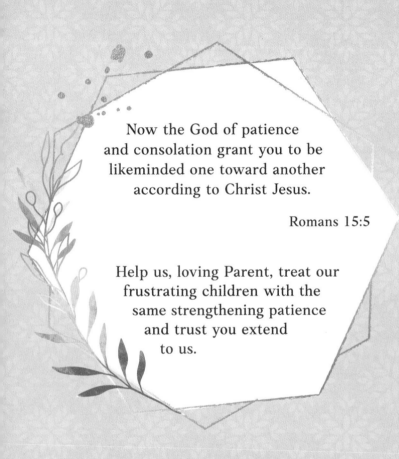

Now the God of patience
and consolation grant you to be
likeminded one toward another
according to Christ Jesus.

Romans 15:5

Help us, loving Parent, treat our
frustrating children with the
same strengthening patience
and trust you extend
to us.

> I will praise thee; for I am fearfully
> and wonderfully made: marvellous
> are thy works; and that
> my soul knoweth right well.
>
> Psalm 139:14

O God, when my child looks at me with
trusting eyes, it gives me a sense of the
incredible power I have in that small
person's life. Give me the guidance and
the wisdom to never take advantage of
that gift. May I never treat my child with
less respect than I would treat myself.
And grant that if I do falter and use this
marvellous life that you have fearfully,
wonderfully made for my own gain,
that you would humble me with the
realization that parenting is not about
cloning but about creating unique persons.

But thou, O Lord, art a shield for me;
my glory, and the lifter up
of mine head.

Psalm 3:3

Lord, a child's fears and anxieties are
a real concern to a mother. We can
usually calm younger children's fears,
but, as they grow older, youngsters are
exposed to horrible sights and sounds
on TV, which can raise terror in the
bravest of us. I can't always control
situations that cause my children to be
afraid, but you can. You can conquer
the mightiest enemy. Lift us up, Lord.
Help us to put to rest some of those
fears and to build in our children a
quiet confidence that you will protect
them. Give them a sense of your
presence, and let them know you are
with them wherever they go.

And on the seventh
day God ended
his work which
he had made;
and he rested
on the seventh day
from all his work which
he had made.

Genesis 2:2

Lord, each day we wage the homework battle
at our house. I have mixed feelings about my
children's homework, Lord. I understand
there is much to learn, but with hours of
homework, the kids have little time for play.
I am sympathetic, but since they must do
the work, I want them to be thorough.
They want to do just enough to "get
by." I trust you to know what is
best for each of them, and I commit
this problem to your care, Father.
Help us to sort
through the
options and
arrive at a good
plan for all, that
mixes work and rest.

The parents brought in the child
Jesus, to do for him after
the custom of the law.

Luke 2:27

This birthday, Lord, my child becomes
a teen. Surely it's just the smoke
of thirteen candles making me cry.
But, O Lord, wasn't it just yesterday
that there was just a single candle?
From before that day to this, I've
trusted you. I ask you now to bless
the youthful drive to risk making
choices; the struggle to be heard;
the changing body, moods, and
mind. Bless—and this is hardest
for me to say—the urge for
independence. Bless me with ears
to listen, a shoulder to lean on,
and the good sense to build bridges,
not walls.

> Be merciful unto me, O God,
> be merciful unto me: for my soul
> trusteth in thee: yea, in the shadow
> of thy wings will I make my refuge,
> until these calamities be overpast.
>
> Psalm 57:1

Almighty God, the world is a fearsome place where violence is glorified, disease is rampant, and young children are victimized daily. I am afraid for my family, but you are our refuge and strength, and we seek protection under the shadow of your wings. Continue to guard my loved ones, Lord: my husband, my children, and all others so dear to me. Preserve them from harm, guard them from the pain of sorrow and suffering, and bless them with good health. In times of trouble, arm us for the battle and guide us safely through it. Our confidence is with you.

But let all those that put their trust
in thee rejoice: let them ever shout
for joy, because thou defendest them:
let them also that love thy name
be joyful in thee.

Psalm 5:11

God bless this joyful life I have been given,
this honor of being called "mother," "wife,"
and "caretaker." God bless my husband,
my children, and my home. God bless
my friends and neighbors and the people I
meet along the way. God bless the joy and
the pain, the pleasure and the frustration.
God bless every moment of it, every load
of laundry, every carpool day, every late
night stolen moment with my spouse,
every phone call that interrupts dinner,
every skinned knee and broken heart.
God bless it all!

Lord, my heart is uplifted as I think
of the special gift you have given me:
a community of faith. I thank you for
my church and for the dear people who
have become part of my support system.
I thank you for your invitation to spend
time with you in trust and fellowship.

My husband and children and I need
the blessings of church attendance.
We need the fellowship and care of
other believers; we need to be refreshed
with the words of scripture and feel the
power of prayer washing over us.
We need to experience your presence,
Lord, in your house, and to become
involved in your work.

Please continue to strengthen our
children's ties to your church so that
they, too, may participate in the joys of
life in the Christian community.

Let him that stole steal no more: but rather let him labour, working with his hands the thing which is good, that he may have to give to him that needeth.

Ephesians 4:28

My 14-year-old son Cal began high school this year. He's always run with a nice group of kids, but this year he drifted into a new crowd and my spouse and I were dismayed to see some changes in his behavior. He stopped taking his schoolwork seriously and his grades dropped. Cal's attitude at home became blasé and sullen. It seemed to be "cool" to not care about school or his family. Worried about the threat of drugs and alcohol, my spouse and I tried various things, from grounding our son and withdrawing privileges to encouraging him to join a club at school. But it was only when my dad introduced Cal to woodworking that we saw some of the old Cal return. Working creatively with his hands seems almost therapeutic for our son. He likes going over to my dad's workshop. He likes creating something that lasts. Cal hasn't been hanging out as much with the new group of friends. He's working on a series of bookshelves for his room. God, thank you for helping us to help Cal. Finding constructive things to do is a great way to re-channel energy that's been misspent.

Let Israel rejoice in him that
made him: let the children
of Zion be joyful
in their King.

Psalm 149:2

Lord, I suppose in every
family there is a child whose
self-esteem suffers by comparison
with siblings. Let me be sensitive
to the subtle messages my children
are receiving within the family
circle, regarding their self-worth.
Help me to show my confidence
in each child and to remind them
all that they matter to our family.
They also matter to you, Lord, for
you are the God who cares for and
values each of your children. Give my
young ones the assurance, the bedrock
trust, that comes with knowing they are
the children of a King.

The spirit of God
hath made me, and the
breath of the Almighty hath
given me life.

Job 33:4

O God, stir new possibilities for our
vibrant family into life among embers
of trust in you. We know the Spirit
fans the flame of growth so that
we may become one with you,
the root from which we,
leaf and folk, have
their source.

> Children's children are the crown
> of old men; and the glory of children
> are their fathers.
>
> Proverbs 17:6

Today, I remember and honor the grandparents who tended us so well. Pause with us as we play again in the dusty lanes of childhood at Grandma and Grandpa's house. Bless these bigger-than-life companions who helped us bridge home and away, childhood and maturity. In their footsteps, we made the journey. Thank you for such a heritage.

As for God, his way is perfect; the word of the Lord is tried: he is a buckler to all them that trust in him.

2 Samuel 22:31

Thank you, God, for your love that makes me part of a community of all those who trust in you. Today I am especially thankful for my family. My parents, my siblings, my cousins and aunts and uncles...all are part of my family and my life. I may not be close to everyone or see everyone as often as I'd like, but I am grateful for their presence in my life. My family is a big part of who I am today. I need to thank them for that gift, even as I thank God for putting these special people in my life.

Thou shalt rise up
before the hoary head,
and honour the face of
the old man,
and fear thy God:
I am the Lord.

Leviticus 19:32

Over the years, my siblings and I have sometimes drifted apart, not through animosity but because we've all been busy with our own immediate families. In dealing with our parents as they age and develop some health problems, we've moved back into a shared orbit. Thank you, God, for that newfound closeness as we navigate these sometimes daunting challenges together. Please help all of us—parents, children, grandchildren—to trust in your goodness.

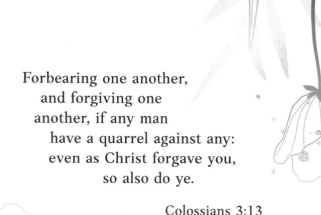

Forbearing one another,
and forgiving one
another, if any man
have a quarrel against any:
even as Christ forgave you,
so also do ye.

Colossians 3:13

Enter and bless this family,
Lord, so that its circle will be
where quarrels are made up
and relationships mature, where
failures are forgiven and new
direction found.

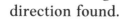

With the ancient is wisdom;
and in length of days understanding.
With him is wisdom and strength,
he hath counsel and understanding.

Job 12:12–13

My parents died when I was barely
out of school, and at first, I proceeded
through life almost blindly. I made my
way as best I could, but sometimes it
was a lonely road. I have learned in the
years since that God puts people into
my path, to help guide me, and when
I remain open, I can benefit from the
knowledge others have to share. Many
of these folks are older than me. They
possess the wisdom born of experience,
and a broad worldview that helps me to
keep perspective. Dear Lord, please may
I always remember to seek instruction
from those who have gone down the
path before me.

There was a man in Jerusalem,
whose name was Simeon;
and the same man was just
and devout, waiting for
the consolation of Israel:
and the Holy Ghost
was upon him.

Luke 2:25

Thank you for our elders, those
grandparents and great-aunts
and uncles who have modeled
faith and generosity to us! Thank
you for those stalwart members
of our faith community who, like
Anna and Simeon, have grown
deep in their faith over their
long lives, acting as a beacon
to us.

> Let us consider one another
> to provoke unto love and
> to good works: Not forsaking
> the assembling of ourselves together,
> as the manner of some is;
> but exhorting one another.
>
> Hebrews 10:24–25

Lord, I cannot thank you enough for my church community. When my husband was laid off unexpectedly last year, our stress levels were high and money was tight. Friends from church invited our kids along to some outings and quietly picked up the tab, helped my husband hone his résumé, and rallied around in prayer. They were there for us during the hard times and they celebrated with us when he found a new job. Please bless them, God, for they demonstrated your love and support to us!

> Be kindly affectioned one to another with brotherly love; in honour preferring one another.
>
> Romans 12:10

Chelsea was blindsided when she learned she had breast cancer, but she and her husband have a strong network of friends who helped with cooking, babysitting, and cleaning during what proved to be a grueling schedule of chemotherapy and radiation. Seven years later, Chelsea is a cancer survivor—and grateful. "My friends had my back; I'll never forget that. They are stellar people, and I try to demonstrate, in my words and actions, how much they mean to me."

Dear God, may I treat my friends with love and honor. I hold them up to you today.

How excellent is thy lovingkindness,
O God! therefore the children
of men put their trust under
the shadow of thy wings.

Psalm 36:7

O God, your love is so great. I'm not sure that I can love as you do or even love others in a way that will please you. God, teach me how to really love my family, my friends, and even strangers. I trust in the power of your love to make me into a far more loving person than I am today. Amen.

For if ye forgive men
their trespasses, your heavenly
Father will also forgive you.

Matthew 6:14

O Christ, our Creator and Redeemer,
Almighty Lord God, forgive the sins
of all who are joined to us by
friendship and relationship,
all for whom we are desired to pray,
or have resolved to pray, and all thy
faithful people. Deliver us
all from evil, preserve us in all good,
and bring us at last to everlasting joy;
for thine honor and glory. Amen.

6th-century prayer

If any of you lack wisdom,
let him ask of God, that giveth to
all men liberally, and upbraideth not;
and it shall be given him.

James 1:5

When my college roommate started acting
erratically, having episodes of mania in which
she talked fast, spent money wildly, and
needed little sleep, followed by bouts of
depression where it was tough to motivate
her to get out of bed and go class, the signs
were familiar. These are the signs my sister
and uncle exhibited before they were
diagnosed with bipolar disorder and sought
treatment. But I know that my family
history of mental illness doesn't make me
a psychiatrist. I want to speak up about my
concerns without risking our friendship.
Lord, please help me find the right words
that will help this situation.

A froward man soweth strife:
and a whisperer separateth
chief friends.

Proverbs 16:28

For several years I've regularly met with a
circle of women to play bunco; I enjoy the
camaraderie and sense of community that
the group provides. Membership has changed
over the years: some folks have moved away,
even as new faces have joined up, and in
many ways that's kept the group from
stagnating. But recently, I've noticed that
the dynamic of the group has changed in a
not-so-positive way. While in the past, talk
focused more on current events, movies, and
books read, lately conversation has turned
more than once to gossip. More distressing
still, I've found myself drawn in, though
afterwards, I invariably feel bad. Lord, please
help me to stay faithful and clear minded.
May I not be distracted by the strife that
comes with gossip; please help me to redirect
idle conversation into a more positive vein.

And oppress not the widow,
nor the fatherless, the stranger,
nor the poor; and let none of you
imagine evil against his brother
in your heart.

Zechariah 7:10

God, I look around my community today and
I feel helpless. The homeless, the hurting,
the needs each one represents are more
than I can handle. But you can do it.
You can meet each need. Teach me.
Strengthen me and use me to serve
as I reach out to my neighbor and
meet Just One Need at a Time!

And when Jesus was come into Peter's house, he saw his wife's mother laid, and sick of a fever. And he touched her hand, and the fever left her: and she arose, and ministered unto them.

Matthew 8:14–15

Bring your cool caress to the foreheads of those suffering fever. By your Spirit, lift the spirits of the bedridden and give comfort to those in pain. Strengthen all entrusted with the care of the infirm today, and give them renewed energy for their tasks. And remind us all that heaven awaits— where we will all be whole and healthy before you, brothers and sisters forever.

And they continued stedfastly
in the apostles' doctrine
and fellowship, and in breaking
of bread, and in prayers.

Acts 2:42

Thank you, God, for those in my life who
are like family...the childhood friend who has
become a sister of the heart, the college friend
who has been an honorary uncle to the kids,
the neighbor who dispenses grandfatherly
wisdom. Thank you for the blessing of love.
Let me, too, open my heart to others, trusting
you to guide me to those you want in my life.

> God setteth the solitary in families:
> he bringeth out those which
> are bound with chains:
> but the rebellious dwell in a dry land.
>
> Psalm 68:6

We are not alone. God sets us in a family, but the family he speaks of here is his own: "A father of the fatherless, and a judge of the widows, is God in his holy habitation" (verse 5). We are adopted into his family, co-heirs with his own son.

The church, then, is the family of God. We care for each other as beloved brothers and sisters, bringing our needs to the Father and keeping the rules of his household. We also marvel at being a part of such a family.

For as the sufferings of Christ
abound in us, so our consolation
also aboundeth by Christ.

2 Corinthians 1:5

God, we know that pain has
produced some wisdom in our
lives, but it has also created
cynicism and fear. People turn
on us, reject us, hurt us, and
none of us wants to play
the fool more than once, so
we're tempted to close off our
hearts to people and to you.
But relationships that bring
meaning and joy require
vulnerability. Help us trust
you to be our truest friend
and to lead us to the kind of
community that will bring
healing rather than destruction.

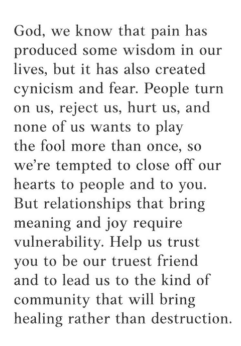

And let the beauty of the
Lord our God be upon us:
and establish thou the work
of our hands upon us; yea,
the work of our hands
establish thou it.

Psalm 90:17

I pray today for people who
work in jobs where they help
others: teachers, firefighters,
EMTs, librarians, caregivers,
medical staff. So many go above
and beyond their official duties
when they see someone in need.
Please keep them safe from burnout.
Please give those who interact with
them a thankful heart.

> He hath shewed thee, O man,
> what is good; and what doth the Lord
> require of thee, but to do justly,
> and to love mercy, and to walk
> humbly with thy God?
>
> Micah 6:8

Dear God, help us to see that none of us are immune to losing ourselves or to hurting one another. Please help us stay on course so we may find our own true essences. Please help us walk in your pathways, trusting only in you and not in our own abilities. Amen.

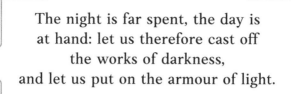

> The night is far spent, the day is
> at hand: let us therefore cast off
> the works of darkness,
> and let us put on the armour of light.
>
> Romans 13:12

Dear God,

I look around and see so many people hurting
one another, and it makes my heart heavy and
sad. What kind of world are we creating for
our children? Why must there be so much
hatred and violence and inhumanity? I pray
for a way to walk through this world without
drowning in sorrow and defeat. I pray for a
light to focus upon when all I hear and see
is dark and bleak. Help me, God, to focus on
the beauty and wonder the world has to offer.
Help me recognize the good and the kind and
the loving. I pray to see beyond my sadness
and despair to the miracles that occur every
day, and to not let my disappointment
overshadow my hope. Amen.

The Lord knoweth the days of
the upright: and their inheritance
shall be for ever. They shall not be
ashamed in the evil time:
and in the days of famine they
shall be satisfied.

Psalm 37:18–19

Lord,

Help me to let go of the chains that
bind me to the people I cannot seem to
forgive. I pray for strength and wisdom
to understand that their sins against me
were because of their own deep fears.
I pray for the guidance to cut the cord
that attaches me to them in anger and
the desire for revenge. Teach me to
forgive others, Lord, as you forgive me,
and to release the poison of resentment
that takes away my peace and serenity.
Teach me to be a better person and to
recognize my own humanity in others,
even as I remove their presence from
my life. Amen.

When thou cuttest down thine
harvest in thy field, and hast forgot
a sheaf in the field, thou shalt not go
again to fetch it: it shall be for the
stranger, for the fatherless,
and for the widow: that the Lord
thy God may bless thee
in all the work of thine hands.

Deuteronomy 24:19

Today I ask you to bless those older
than me. Keep their minds sharp and
their bodies vigorous. Let those who
have caregivers be treated kindly,
with patience and respect. Let those
around them listen, appreciating their
hard-earned wisdom.

> Nor height, nor depth, nor any other creature, shall be able to separate us from the love of God, which is in Christ Jesus our Lord.
>
> Romans 8:39

This is not a choice I would make, for me or for the one who went against my standards, my hopes. It's a riddle, O God, why you give us freedom to choose. It can break our hearts. Comfort me as I cope with a choice not mine; forgive any role I had in it. Help me separate doer from deed as I pass on your words to all: "...nothing can separate us." Not even poor choices I sometimes make myself.

But as for me, I will walk
in mine integrity: redeem me,
and be merciful unto me.

Psalm 26:11

The sting of rejection lingers long after it has
been inflicted. It often creates an aversion to
drawing near to the very thing that can bring
healing: love through a relationship with God.
It takes a certain willingness to risk reaching
out to be forgiven by God if we ever hope to
find wholeness again. But there is no more
worthwhile risk than that which risks for the
sake of God's love.

Wherefore I say unto
thee, Her sins, which
are many, are forgiven;
for she loved much:
but to whom little is forgiven,
the same loveth little.

Luke 7:47

Dear God, the wound between
this person and me seems too
deep to heal, and the chasm of
misunderstanding seems too
wide to leap across. I pray for
guidance that I may do my part
to close the wound and narrow
the gap between us with love,
understanding, trust, and
forgiveness. Amen.

And his lord was wroth, and delivered
him to the tormentors, till he should
pay all that was due unto him.
So likewise shall my heavenly Father
do also unto you, if ye from your hearts
forgive not every one his brother
their trespasses.

Matthew 18:34–35

God, I pray for the strength and the wisdom
to know what to do in this situation. I pray
for enough love to forgive this person for the
pain they have caused me and to forgive
myself for the ill will I have harbored against
this person. Help me be a truly forgiving
person so that the weight of resentment may
be lifted from my shoulders. Amen.

Bring forth therefore fruits
worthy of repentance.

Luke 3:8

Lord God, the words "I'm
sorry" and "forgive me" have
got to be the most powerful
in our vocabulary. May these
phrases ever be poised on my
lips, ready to do their work
of release and restoration.
Let your healing balm wash
over me, Father, as I both grant
and receive the freedom that
forgiveness brings. I trust you
to heal me. Thank you. Amen.

Take heed to yourselves: If thy brother trespass against thee, rebuke him; and if he repent, forgive him. And if he trespass against thee seven times in a day, and seven times in a day turn again to thee, saying, I repent; thou shalt forgive him.

Luke 17:3–4

Lord, I need you to help me with the concept of forgiving people over and over again for the same behavior. I know you taught that there was no limit to the number of times we should forgive someone, but I get so weary of doing it, Lord, and I don't always trust that it will work out well. Help me to have a heart of forgiveness, so ready to forgive that I do so before the person who has wronged me even seeks my forgiveness. There's freedom in that kind of forgiveness, Lord. Help me claim it for my own. Amen.

> There is neither Jew nor Greek,
> there is neither bond nor free,
> there is neither male nor female:
> for ye are all one in Christ Jesus.
>
> Galatians 3:28

Whether we admit it or not, we all long to feel welcomed and accepted by others. Just as Jesus connected with people outside his circle of disciples, we need to connect with people outside our comfort zone and mirror God's acceptance of all people. Lord, please help me see past any distrust or preconceived notions, seeing with your eyes of love.

ACCEPTING GOD'S PLANS

And we know that all things work together for good to them that love God, to them who are the called according to his purpose.

Romans 8:28

> For my thoughts are not
> your thoughts, neither are your ways
> my ways, saith the Lord.
> For as the heavens are higher than
> the earth, so are my ways higher than
> your ways, and my thoughts than
> your thoughts.
>
> Isaiah 55:8–9

No one knows the mind of God, nor why he chooses to work the way he does. But in our most difficult circumstances, we will miss the peace of his presence unless we persevere in trusting that he is always faithful and always good.

But unto you that fear my name
shall the Sun of righteousness arise
with healing in his wings;
and ye shall go forth, and grow up
as calves of the stall.

Malachi 4:2

I need answers, for I want you to help me heal. But if you send illness, how can I trust you to heal? Reassure me that you will work everything out eventually. And when that isn't possible, be with me as I suffer. Freed from fear I can get stronger as your healing energy flows through me, restoring me to my abundant life.

When Jesus heard that, he said,
This sickness is not unto death,
but for the glory of God,
that the Son of God
might be glorified thereby.

John 11:4

Heavenly Spirit, I long to be healed
from my affliction, but I trust your
will, your timing, and your plan for
my life. I know that you will never
give me more than I can handle and
that you will always be there to help
me. For this I am eternally grateful.
Amen.

And as for me, thou upholdest me in mine integrity, and settest me before thy face for ever.

Psalm 41:12

When we think of integrity, we think of someone who is honorable and trustworthy —a person who keeps their word and guards their reputation. To be called a man or woman of integrity is a high compliment. Such a person knows the difference between right and wrong and diligently pursues doing right, no matter what the obstacles. Jesus provides the best example of a man of integrity; he was not swayed by outer influences but lived a life above reproach. Integrity comes not just from the pursuit of right living, but the pursuit of God, which leads to right living. Let me always trust in your plans, Lord, and follow them with integrity.

Give therefore thy servant
an understanding heart to judge
thy people, that I may discern
between good and bad:
for who is able to judge this thy
so great a people?

1 Kings 3:9

Lord, this is one of those days
when I really don't know which
way to turn. I've lost my sense
of direction and feel as if I'm
sitting on a rock in the forest,
wondering which trail will take
me back to familiar ground. Lead
me, Lord. Send the signs I need to
follow to get where you want me to
go. I put my trust in you.

> For I know that my redeemer liveth,
> and that he shall stand
> at the latter day upon the earth.
>
> Job 19:25

Lord, if my world were turned upside down in a single day like Job's was—losing everything I owned, and far worse, all of my children being killed by a natural disaster— I doubt worship would be my instinctive response. But here is Job, recognizing himself as a mere man and praising you because you are God. He trusts your wisdom that reaches above and beyond his overwhelming tragedy. Somehow, he is able to understand that the blessings you gave him are not his to hold on to or his that he can demand repayment from you. Even Job's punishing trials could not shake his faith and trust in you.

And Mary said,
Behold the handmaid of the Lord;
be it unto me according to thy word.

Luke 1:38

When she said these words, Mary
was carrying the promised Messiah.
The days ahead would not be easy
for Mary. How would she explain
things to her parents and to Joseph?
Was she afraid of how she would be
treated by her friends and neighbors,
as it would appear that she had been
unfaithful? Mary was likely confused
and somewhat frightened, but she
did not fret. She trusted in the Lord
and rejoiced. She praised God for the
honor of being chosen to serve him
in this unique way.

Then I will give you rain in due season, and the land shall yield her increase, and the trees of the field shall yield their fruit.

Leviticus 26:4

Thank you for rain! Not only do April showers bring May flowers, as the old saying goes, but rain can be beautiful in its own right. Thank you for gray days and the sound of rain on the rooftop. Thank you when the basement stays dry. Thank you even when a sports event or outdoor party is canceled—when we let those things happen with calm and acceptance, we find out that your plans for us are better than our own.

And when Jesus had cried with a loud voice, he said, Father, into thy hands I commend my spirit: and having said thus, he gave up the ghost.

Luke 23:46

You gave us the incredible gift of your son, Father God. Thank you.

What do I need to put in your hands?

What do I need to release to you?

With what do I need to trust you?

Then Nebuchadnezzar spake,
and said, Blessed be the God
of Shadrach, Meshach,
and Abednego, who hath sent
his angel, and delivered
his servants that trusted in him,
and have changed the king's
word, and yielded their bodies,
that they might not serve
nor worship any god, except
their own God.

Daniel 3:28

O thou, from whom
all blessings flow,
I lift my heart to thee;
In all my sorrows,
conflicts, woes,
Dear Lord, remember me.
Amen.

Traditional prayer

> For whosoever exalteth himself
> shall be abased; and he that
> humbleth himself shall be exalted.
>
> Luke 14:11

Today, when I am tempted to put myself
first, Lord, remind me of what Jesus said:
you will exalt the humble. You will do it in
your time and in your way, of course, but
I don't have to scramble around and push
ahead to find your blessing and provision.
Help me wait, and be silent, and trust you.
This is a spiritual calculus I don't always
understand. But you have the right answer.
And that's enough.

> For which of you, intending to build a
> tower, sitteth not down first,
> and counteth the cost, whether
> he have sufficient to finish it?
>
> Luke 14:28

My spouse and I recently bought our first house, a little brick bungalow with beautiful bay windows. We've lived in apartments up until now, and suddenly we are homeowners, with all that entails: a postage-stamp-sized yard, a room we can use as an office, and even a guest room. It's been exciting to transform the little bungalow from a house into our home, and we've spent time and money in our efforts to do so. There are many more things we'd like to do—the current light fixture in the dining room is pretty ugly, for instance, and we'd like to replace it—but we work hard for our income, and know we need to pace ourselves financially. As my spouse reminded me the other day, God instructs us to plan carefully down to the last detail, and calculate the costs of everything we do. The new light fixture is going to have to wait, but in the meantime, we are wise to be happy with the fruits of our labors—the blessing of a new home.

God, I know you're not in a hurry—
Your plans for me are on time.
You need no schedule or reminders
for I'm always on your mind.

I know you have drawn the mosaic
and you're fitting each tile in place.
As I continue to follow your plan,
help me not to hurry or race.

So as my life's pattern continues
and the next part begins to unfold,
it's you I'm trusting and praising,
it's your hand I cling to and hold.

Peace is about releasing.
It's about opening my hand
and letting go of my plan,
my agenda,
my demands
on God and other people
and even on myself.
It's about realizing
that every person
is as important as I am
in God's eyes.
It's remembering
I don't know everything
and I don't have solutions
to every problem.
It's about calling on
the One who does.

In the beginning God created
the heaven and the earth.
And the earth was without
form, and void; and darkness
was upon the face of the deep.
And the Spirit of God moved
upon the face of the waters.
And God said, Let there
be light: and there was light.

Genesis 1:1–3

At the dawn of creation,
God laid out his plans
for the universe,
and the plan is still working.

The mind is like a garden of fertile soil into which the seeds of our thoughts, ideas, and intentions are planted. With loving care and nurturing attention, those seeds bloom forth to manifest in our lives as wonderful opportunities and events. Those seeds that we choose to either ignore or neglect will simply die off. Thus, our mind constantly turns over old growth into new. It is where we focus our energy and give our love that breaks through the dark soil into the light of day. It then becomes the visible good in our life, casting off new seeds to one day bloom forth in a cycle of renewal and abundance.

And if it seem evil unto you to serve
the Lord, choose you this day
whom ye will serve; whether the gods
which your fathers served that were
on the other side of the flood,
or the gods of the Amorites, in whose
land ye dwell: but as for me and
my house, we will serve the Lord.

Joshua 24:15

Bless all that happens here, O God, planner
and builder. May we find laughter and love
and strength and sanctuary, and may this be a
house of service to you. Bless all who visit our
love-built home, family and companions with
whom we can grow. May we, like you, offer
shelter and welcome.

And there shall be a tabernacle
for a shadow in the day time
from the heat, and for a place of refuge,
and for a covert from storm
and from rain.

Isaiah 4:6

May you be assured of God's presence
as you weather this storm. As the waves
toss you about, and the ship of your life
threatens to crash into rough rocks:
He is there. Never despair. For no wind
or water, rock or sand has the power to
defeat his plans for you. And, after all,
he created all these things, and in him
alone they have their existence.

But we all, with open face beholding as
in a glass the glory of the Lord,
are changed into the same image
from glory to glory, even as by
the Spirit of the Lord.

2 Corinthians 3:18

In this time of change, help me to be patient
and trust, God. Let me not run ahead of you
and your plans. Give me courage to do only
what is before me and to keep my focus on
my responsibilities. I am tempted to daydream
about the future; however, the future is in
your hands. Thus, may I be close to you in all
my thoughts, accomplish the task before me
today, and do it with all my heart.

> By faith Moses, when he was come
> to years, refused to be called the son
> of Pharaoh's daughter; Choosing
> rather to suffer affliction with
> the people of God, than to enjoy
> the pleasures of sin for a season.
>
> Hebrews 11:24–25

Father God, when I'm tempted to give up on a task or a ministry opportunity, it helps to read about Abraham, Moses, Joseph, David, Job—all those whose times of trial and perseverance are so beautifully preserved for us through your Word. Once we become attuned to your plan for our lives, we can continue on with the certainty that you always complete what you start. We can stand firmly on your promises, confident that you will give us the strength we need to keep going. Thank you for the faith of the ages, Lord! It is also the faith for today.

Abide in me, and I in you. As the branch cannot bear fruit of itself, except it abide in the vine; no more can ye, except ye abide in me.

John 15:4

Lord, I deeply desire to abide in you. I desire to have you abiding in me as well, so closely that I can speak to you any time and feel your presence. Destroy the distractions that create distance between us, Lord. Clear out the clutter that keeps me from sensing your best plan for my life and trusting that you will meet my deepest needs. Then when I ask for what I wish, it will be the fulfillment of your desire for me as well.

> My doctrine shall drop as the rain,
> my speech shall distil as the dew,
> as the small rain upon
> the tender herb, and as the showers
> upon the grass.
>
> Deuteronomy 32:2

Heavenly Father, talking to others about you isn't always easy. It's hard for me to express my emotions in mere words. Though I long to tell my children all you mean to me, self-consciousness gets in the way. Help me to speak to them from my heart and trust that they will hear your truths. Inspire me with language that will fall on fertile soil. Lord, may I be like Moses as I teach my children about you, with words as welcome as the rain and dew on thirsty plants.

The prophet Elisha wants to do something special for a woman who has continuously blessed his ministry. When he asks what she would like, she tells him that there is nothing she needs. Elisha does a little research and finds that she never had a son; he then tells the woman that she will give birth to a son in one year's time.

Instead of rejoicing, the woman cries in fear. Her hope for a son died long ago, and she's terrified to expose herself to more heartbreak.

The weight of hope can be heavy on our souls, and many times we will want to give up on our dreams. But until our yearnings change or subside, we must keep our hope and trust in God's timing and plans. It is okay to raise our hopes in a God who can perform miracles.

Shew me thy ways, O Lord;
teach me thy paths.

Psalm 25:4

How often do we make plans,
only to have them fall apart?
When my day doesn't turn out
the way I planned, it's easy
to become angry. Instead, I
look for ways to make the day
special in a different way and
thank God for showing me a
new path. Lord, teach me to
have a trusting, flexible heart
and be willing to spend my
time as you see fit, not as I do,
and to open my eyes to the
beauty of the unexpected.

I press toward the mark for the prize of the high calling of God in Christ Jesus.

Philippians 3:14

God has a mighty vision for my life, and I plan to live up to those expectations. Through the work I do, and the love I give, I hope to fulfill God's legacy of good in the world. I refuse to stay small when God is asking me to go big.

Thou shalt go to all that
I shall send thee, and
whatsoever I command
thee thou shalt speak.

Jeremiah 1:7

I align my plans with
God's will for my life.
I listen to his guidance
and follow his lead. I
take the steps he directs
me to take, and face the
lessons he asks me to
learn. I trust. I evolve. I
grow. I become!

Thou compassest my path
and my lying down, and art
acquainted with all my ways.

Psalm 139:3

Father God, watch over me as I begin this new journey. I made my plans and created a blueprint for change. I now ask your help carrying it out in the world. Guide me along and help me adjust my path when my plans don't always pan out the way I hoped. Amen.

Therefore if any man
be in Christ,
he is a new creature:
old things are
passed away;
behold, all things are
become new.

2 Corinthians 5:17

God, I know that you
close some doors in my
life in order to open new
ones. I know that things
change and come to an
end in order to leave room
for new beginnings. Help
me have the boldness and
enthusiasm to let go of the
old and accept the new in
trusting faith. Amen.

But Moses hands were heavy;
and they took a stone, and put it
under him, and he sat thereon;
and Aaron and Hur stayed up his hands,
the one on the one side, and the other
on the other side; and his hands were
steady until the going down of the sun.

Exodus 17:12

God, help me to accept the help I need and to give up my stubborn need to control the outcome of every situation. Show me that sometimes my will is not always the best and that sometimes you send us healing angels in the form of other humans. Thank you. Amen.

Wherefore seeing we also are
compassed about with so great
a cloud of witnesses, let us lay aside
every weight, and the sin which
doth so easily beset us, and let us run
with patience the race that
is set before us.

Hebrews 12:1

God, please help me to accept your
itinerary for my life's journey no matter
where it brings me. I will wait for you
to decide when I should return to your
home. Amen.

And they said one to another,
Did not our heart burn within us,
while he talked with us by the way,
and while he opened to us
the scriptures?

Luke 24:32

Father God, we know that to receive the blessing of healing, the heart must be open. But when we are mad, we close off the heart as if it were a prison. Remind us that a heart that is shut cannot receive understanding, acceptance, and renewal. Even though we feel angry, we must keep the heart's door slightly ajar so your grace can enter and fill our darkness with the light of hope.

Like the littered house in the aftermath of the holidays, my soul is overcrowded. What, I worry, do I need to be a good parent?

Guide my sorting. Keep humor; toss battles of will. Keep tolerance and imagination; toss inflexibility and overreactive fear. Keep respect and acceptance of kids just as they are today; toss supermom lists and myths and others' expectations.

Guided by you, O God, my sorting will continue as I toss out useless worrying habits.

And he said unto him,
If now I have found grace
in thy sight, then shew me
a sign that thou talkest
with me.

Judges 6:17

To those scanning a night
sky, you sent a star. To
those tending sheep on
a silent hill, you sent a
voice. What sign, Lord,
are you sending me to
come, be, and do all you
intend? Let me hear, see,
trust, and accept it when
you do.

And the Lord, he it is that doth go before thee; he will be with thee, he will not fail thee, neither forsake thee: fear not, neither be dismayed.

Deuteronomy 31:8

Lord, sometimes I get frustrated, especially when I have to face something new. Thank you for giving me an open heart. Help me accept change and rejoice in new experiences and new people. Help me to be grateful for new opportunities and always see the good things even when I am afraid to try something new.

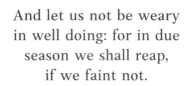

And let us not be weary
in well doing: for in due
season we shall reap,
if we faint not.

Galatians 6:9

When I operate from my
own will, I grow tired
and weary. When I trust
and accept God's will, I
feel as though the flood-
gates have opened and I
am floating downstream,
relaxed and in the flow
of blessings!

As for God, his way is perfect:
the word of the Lord is tried:
he is a buckler to all those that
trust in him.

Psalm 18:30

Life goes back and forth between push and pull, force and acceptance, fight and surrender. It's exhausting! But staying in God's will makes the doors of life open easier and more frequently than when we rely only on ourselves.

Blessed are the poor in spirit:
for theirs is the kingdom
of heaven.

Matthew 5:3

I want to be independent,
self-reliant, and competent.
I want to be talented. But
without you, God, I have
nothing. Please never let me
forget that any gift that I
have comes from you. Please
help me let go of all things
that are not from you, and
accept with humility my
dependence on you.

As every man hath received the gift,
even so minister the same one
to another, as good stewards
of the manifold grace of God.

1 Peter 4:10

All our opportunities, abilities, and resources come from God. They are given to us to hold in sacred trust for him. Cooperating with God will permit us to generously pass on to others some of the many blessings from his rich storehouse.

> Put on therefore, as the elect of God, holy and beloved, bowels of mercies, kindness, humbleness of mind, meekness, longsuffering.
>
> Colossians 3:12

Kindness sows a seed within me that begins to sprout where before all was barren. Leaves of trust start to bud, and I branch out. I take in gentle caring and loving nudging and realize I might just go ahead and bloom! After all, God arranged spring after winter.

For thus saith the Lord God, the Holy One of Israel; In returning and rest shall ye be saved; in quietness and in confidence shall be your strength.

Isaiah 30:15

Hold fast to your belief in yourself, and God's belief in you. Do this one thing, and you can do anything, achieve anything! Never waver in trusting that you are being guided and directed. Go for it!

Follow peace with all men, and holiness, without which no man shall see the Lord.

Hebrews 12:14

God wants us to know peace is in every area of our lives— peace in our daily work, our business, our family, our soul. The key to letting peace enter in is to invite God into each of these areas daily.

Forasmuch as ye are manifestly
declared to be the epistle of
Christ ministered by us,
written not with ink,
but with the Spirit of the living God;
not in tables of stone,
but in fleshy tables of the heart.
And such trust have
we through Christ to God-ward:
Not that we are sufficient of ourselves
to think any thing as of ourselves;
but our sufficiency is of God

2 Corinthians 3:3–5

Dear Lord, help me to build on a firm
foundation by relying on your wisdom,
diligently seeking your direction in all I do,
learning to walk in your paths of kindness,
peace, and justice to my neighbors. In
Jesus' name, Amen.

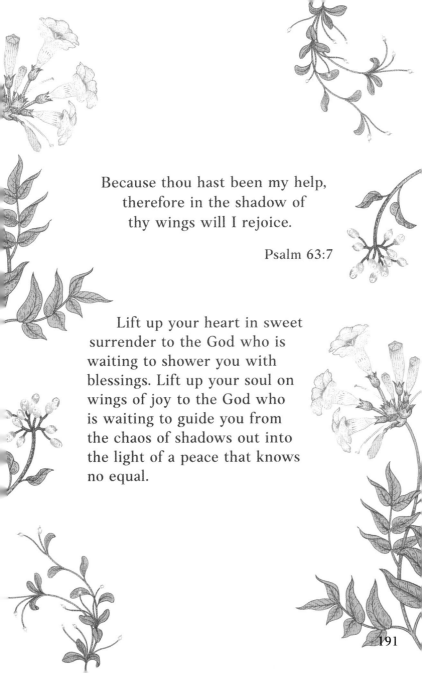

Because thou hast been my help,
therefore in the shadow of
thy wings will I rejoice.

Psalm 63:7

Lift up your heart in sweet
surrender to the God who is
waiting to shower you with
blessings. Lift up your soul on
wings of joy to the God who
is waiting to guide you from
the chaos of shadows out into
the light of a peace that knows
no equal.

Some trust in chariots,
and some in horses:
but we will remember
the name of the Lord
our God.

Psalm 20:7

God, when life feels
like a ride that won't
let us off, remind us
that you are waiting for
us to reach up to you.
And when we finally
do, thank you for being
there to lift us to peace
and safety.

Open up my heavy heart,
that surely day by day,
the bitterness and wrath in me
will slowly drain away.
God let your spirit enter in
and fill each empty space
with peace and healing to my soul
through your unending grace.

But the fruit of the Spirit is love,
joy, peace, longsuffering, gentleness,
goodness, faith, meekness, temperance:
against such there is no law.

Galatians 5:22–23

Lord, how I pray that your love is evident in me today! I want to follow you closely and help draw others to you as well. I know that if those with whom I come in contact see love, joy, peace, patience, kindness, goodness, faithfulness, gentleness, and self-control in me, they may find you as well. Direct my steps as I follow you, Lord, and may the grace you've sprinkled on me be revealed for your glory. Amen.

That we should be to the praise
of his glory, who first trusted
in Christ. In whom ye also trusted,
after that ye heard the word of truth,
the gospel of your salvation.

Ephesians 1:12–13

Thank you for your wise ways, Lord.
Following them fills my life with true
blessings—the riches of love and
relationship, joy and provision, peace
and protection. I remember reading
in your Word that whenever I ask for
your wisdom from a faith-filled heart,
you will give it, no holds barred. So
I'll ask once again today for your
insight and understanding as I build,
using your blueprints.

TRUST AND
COMFORT

But Jesus turned him about,
and when he saw her, he said,
Daughter, be of good comfort;
thy faith hath made thee whole.

Matthew 9:22

> The people which sat in darkness
> saw great light; and to them
> which sat in the region and shadow
> of death light is sprung up.
>
> Matthew 4:16

Teach us to know and trust, God, that it is exactly at the point of our deepest despair that you are closest. For at those times we can finally admit we have wandered in the dark, without a clue. Yet you have been there with us all along. Thank you for your abiding presence.

Comfort ye, comfort ye
my people, saith your God.

Isaiah 40:1

God promises us his comfort,
but he also uses us as his
agents to comfort others. In
fact, the difficulties we've
gone through often give us the
ability to reassure others who
are now going through the
same experiences. How will
God use you to extend comfort
to someone else?

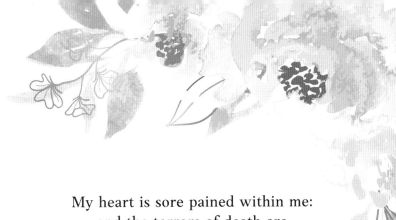

My heart is sore pained within me:
and the terrors of death are
fallen upon me.

Psalm 55:4

Why is there so much pain in
the world, God? It's so hard to
understand. Lord, help us through
it all. Help us comprehend or at
least simply trust in you.

Cast thy burden upon the Lord,
and he shall sustain thee:
he shall never suffer the righteous
to be moved.

Psalm 55:22

We have seen that inconceivable acts can cause our world to crumble around us. Yet we need not fall apart inside. If we place our trust in God's goodness, he will come to our aid and bring us comfort to restore our hope in the future. His love and compassion will lift our spirits so we can rejoice no matter what disaster or tragedy may befall us. For as long as God is beside us, nothing can defeat us or take what is truly important from us.

O my God, I trust in thee: let me not be ashamed, let not mine enemies triumph over me.

Psalm 25:2

Disasters strike. No time to prepare. Help us, Lord, stay close to you. Deepen our trust and faith in you. Amen.

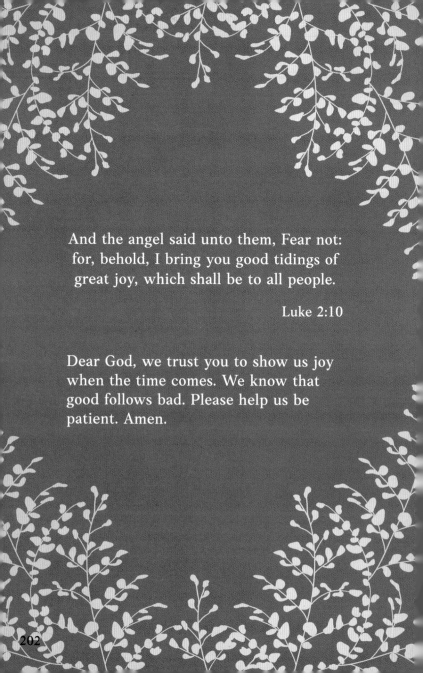

And the angel said unto them, Fear not: for, behold, I bring you good tidings of great joy, which shall be to all people.

Luke 2:10

Dear God, we trust you to show us joy when the time comes. We know that good follows bad. Please help us be patient. Amen.

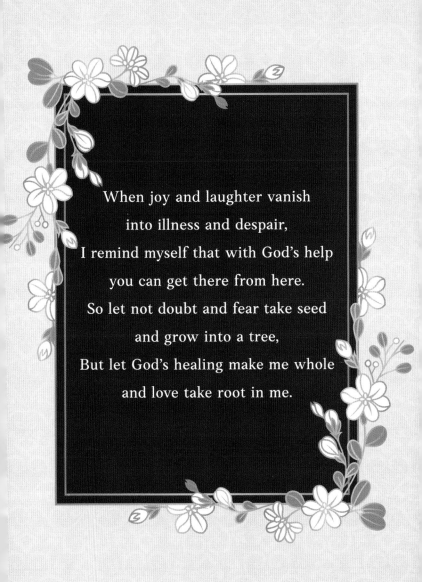

When joy and laughter vanish
into illness and despair,
I remind myself that with God's help
you can get there from here.
So let not doubt and fear take seed
and grow into a tree,
But let God's healing make me whole
and love take root in me.

Blessed are they whose
iniquities are forgiven,
and whose sins are covered.

Romans 4:7

God, I do not intend to hurt
you and others. I am not
always sure what happens in
those times when I do hurt
you and others. I am thankful
that you forgive. Please help
others to forgive me, too.
Remind us all to follow your
teachings. We pray that you
will guide and comfort us.

> Then Jonah prayed unto the Lord his
> God out of the fish's belly,
> and said, I cried by reason
> of mine affliction unto the Lord,
> and he heard me;
> out of the belly of hell cried I,
> and thou heardest my voice.
>
> Jonah 2:1–2

I cry out to you, O Lord, from the belly of my fear. In this dark pit of anxiety and confusion over my health, I ask that you reach in and guide me into the light of day. My faith in you is strong, and my trust in you is steadfast. Come to my aid, O Lord, as you did when Jonah called to you. Amen.

Again I will build thee,
and thou shalt be built,
O virgin of Israel: thou shalt again
be adorned with thy tabrets,
and shalt go forth in the dances
of them that make merry.

Jeremiah 31:4

In the aftermath of tragedy, it takes energy and courage to rebuild, Great Architect. How amazing that your gift of courage translates worry into energy and fear into determination. Help us recognize ill feelings as potential fuel that can be turned into reconstruction tools. Through your grace, we've courageously faced what was our lives and we are now off to see what our lives can be.

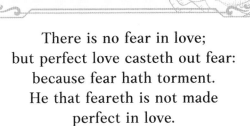

There is no fear in love;
but perfect love casteth out fear:
because fear hath torment.
He that feareth is not made
perfect in love.

1 John 4:18

God of All Comfort, I trust that with you by my side I am never alone. Your perfect love casts out all fear, doubt, and uncertainty. Your presence emboldens and empowers me. You are the light that leads me to safety again. Amen.

But all God's angels
come to us disguised;
Sorrow and sickness,
poverty and death,
One after the other
lift their frowning masks,
And we behold the Seraph's
face beneath,
All the radiant with
the glory and the calm
of having looked upon
the front of God.

James Russell Lowell,
"Death of a Friend's Child"

Even the Spirit of truth;
whom the world cannot receive,
because it seeth him not,
neither knoweth him: but ye
know him; for he dwelleth
with you, and shall be in you.
I will not leave you comfortless:
I will come to you.
Yet a little while, and the world
seeth me no more;
but ye see me: because I live,
ye shall live also.

John 14:17–19

The comfort of the Lord is truly
trustworthy.

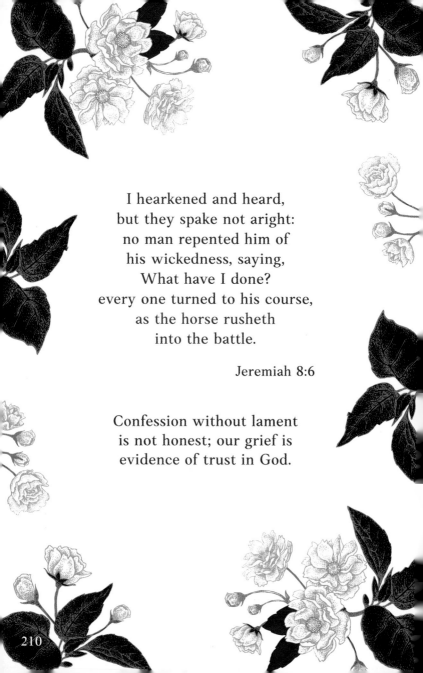

I hearkened and heard,
but they spake not aright:
no man repented him of
his wickedness, saying,
What have I done?
every one turned to his course,
as the horse rusheth
into the battle.

Jeremiah 8:6

Confession without lament
is not honest; our grief is
evidence of trust in God.

We glory in tribulations also: knowing that tribulation worketh patience.

Romans 5:3

God of all comfort, have mercy on me. I got angry today at my husband and accused him of not helping me enough. I scolded my child for talking too much. I shouted at the dog for barking too loud. And I almost hung up on my neighbor for taking up too much of my time with her plumbing problems. I need your comforting strength, dear God, wrapped around me like a soothing blanket, so that I can ask my family for forgiveness. Bless me with more patience, too, so that we don't have to go through all this again tomorrow. Thank you, God.

But I will sing of thy power;
yea, I will sing aloud of thy mercy
in the morning: for thou hast been
my defence and refuge in the day
of my trouble.

Psalm 59:16

When the winds of change and challenge
blow hard into my life, I will take refuge in
you, O Lord. When the darkness descends
upon my house and home, I will fear not,
for I will place my faith in you, O Lord.
When my child is ill or my husband is hurt,
I will remain steadfast, for I know that
you will be right there by my side, O Lord.
Although I cannot see you, I trust you are
always with me, O Lord, and in that I take
comfort and find strength.

Take comfort in God's
steadfast presence.
Even when you suffer,
take comfort
in the hope of God's healing.
Even when you fear,
take comfort
in the hope of God's strength.
No matter what you face,
take comfort
in knowing you never
walk alone.

I am the good shepherd:
the good shepherd giveth his life
for the sheep.

John 10:11

O Lord Jesus Christ, thou, good Shepherd
of the sheep, who camest to seek the lost,
and to gather them to thy fold, have
compassion upon those who have
wandered from thee; feed those who
hunger, cause the weary to lie down
in thy pastures, bind up those who are
broken in heart, and strengthen those who
are weak, that we, relying on thy care
and being comforted by thy love,
may abide in thy guidance to our
lives' end; for thy name's sake. Amen.

6th-century prayer

> In my distress I cried unto the Lord,
> and he heard me.
>
> Psalm 120:1

This is a Psalm of Ascent, a song Jesus sang on the roads from Galilee to Jerusalem as a young boy. And the promise it suggests is one he believed as he prayed to his Father in the garden of Gethsemane on the night of his betrayal. When we cry to the Lord, he hears us.

There is comfort in this, even if the Father's will is different from ours. "O my Father, if this cup may not pass away from me, except I drink it, thy will be done," Jesus prayed (Matthew 26:42). The Father's will was that he would die. Yet we also know that "there appeared an angel unto him from heaven, strengthening him" (Luke 22:43). Yes, the Father heard him. That was the promise.

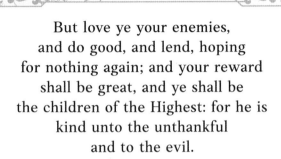

But love ye your enemies,
and do good, and lend, hoping
for nothing again; and your reward
shall be great, and ye shall be
the children of the Highest: for he is
kind unto the unthankful
and to the evil.

Luke 6:35

When we see our enemies from God's perspective, compassion follows, for he has seen the sorrows in their hearts that have caused them to behave in such a manner. He longs to reach out to these people and comfort them, and he sometimes uses our hands to do it.

Come unto me,
all ye that labour and are heavy laden,
and I will give you rest.

Matthew 11:28

Lord, people I love are going through
a hard and stressful time. Please help
them, comfort them, and bring them
peace and sweet, pain-free sleep. Ease
the tension in their bodies and the
ache in their hearts. Heal their hurts,
please, Lord, and let them rest easy.

Be not a terror unto me:
thou art my hope in the day of evil.

Jeremiah 17:17

God's grace is our comfort in times of
trouble and our beacon of hope amid the
blackness of despair. By opening ourselves
to God's ever-present grace and trust in
it, we know we are loved and cared for,
and our hearts sing out in joyful gratitude.

I will both lay me down
in peace, and sleep: for thou,
Lord, only makest me dwell
in safety.

Psalm 4:8

Reach out to me, a child again,
lost, frightened, and alone with
few answers for comfort. Stay
with me until I fall asleep and
be here if I awake scared.
Let me be a child tonight, Lord.
Tomorrow I'll be big and strong
and all grown up, but for now,
find me, hold me.

Rejoice with them that do rejoice,
and weep with them that weep.

Romans 12:15

I sit in what once was and grieve what is lost forever. And yet words once heard float like mind-perfume, opening up a floodgate of memory, recalling the moments when those words were spoken. And I am comforted. Thank you, O God, for the gift of remembering.

> Thus saith the Lord; Cursed be
> the man that trusteth in man,
> and maketh flesh his arm, and whose
> heart departeth from the Lord.
>
> Jeremiah 17:5

At age four, my brother believed he could outrun any car because the soles of his new sandals looked like tire tread. "Watch me!" he shouted over his shoulder as he dashed down a hill at the summer camp where we were vacationing. Just then he took a nasty spill, cutting his knee and injuring his pride. As he wailed, my parents rushed over to comfort him.

How like that little boy I can be: Look, God, I'm all ready to do great things for you. I've got all the right credentials and intentions. Just watch me! Then fwomp! Down I go. But even while my wounds are stinging and my pride is still smarting, there is God comforting me, and his very presence brings me back to my senses, back to the humble dependence on him once again.

> For God sent not his Son
> into the world to condemn the world;
> but that the world through him
> might be saved.
>
> John 3:17

Dear Father God, you sent your son to us to be our Lord, to watch over us, to bring us comfort, strength, hope, and healing when our hearts are broken and our lives seem shattered. We will never be alone, not when you are here with us always and forever. Remind us to look to you for strength. Amen.

And whether we be afflicted,
it is for your consolation and salvation,
which is effectual in the enduring
of the same sufferings
which we also suffer:
or whether we be comforted,
it is for your consolation and salvation.

2 Corinthians 1:6

Lord, we trust that you do not leave us to suffer alone. You are with us in pain, in sickness, and in our worst moments. Thank you for your comfort and healing power. Thank you for getting us through when our bodies fail, when our health falters, and when we need you most of all. Amen.

Thou wilt surely wear away, both thou, and this people that is with thee: for this thing is too heavy for thee; thou art not able to perform it thyself alone.

Exodus 18:18

While I wait for this piercing pain of loneliness to pass, Great Comforter, cradle me as the wailing, lost child I've become. Closing my eyes and breathing deeply, I feel your warming presence as a blanket tossed around my shoulders and know that no matter how lost I feel right now, you hold the most important truth, whispering it now: "You are my beloved child. I am with you."

Why art thou
thus cast down,
my heart?
Why troubled,
why dost mourn apart,
O'er nought
but earthly wealth?
Trust in thy God,
be not afraid,
He is thy Friend
who all things made.

Hans Sachs, trans.
Catherine Winkworth

225

A time to be born, and a time to die;
a time to plant, and a time to pluck up
that which is planted; A time to kill,
and a time to heal; a time to break down,
and a time to build up; A time to weep,
and a time to laugh; a time to mourn,
and a time to dance.

Ecclesiastes 3:2–4

You are everywhere, Lord, and we're
comforted to be enfolded as we move
through life's extremes. You are with us
in birthings and dyings, in routine and
surprise, and in stillness and activity.
We cannot wander so far in any direction
that you are not already there.

> Trust in the Lord, and do good;
> so shalt thou dwell in the land,
> and verily thou shalt be fed.
>
> Psalm 37:3

Are you here, Lord? I've never felt lonelier than in this illness. Sometimes I feel easier saying a child's prayer or repeating a familiar verse—anything to connect with you. Hear me, O God, for I feel like a stranger.

I'm comforted, for just the simple act of praying reminds me you are in the middle of not only the illness, but also the getting well. You are where you're needed, my steadfast companion.

> What time I am afraid,
> I will trust in thee.
>
> Psalm 56:3

Just when I settle in with one reality, something new disrupts. Overnight change, God of all the time in the world, is comforting and grief-making, for it's a reminder that nothing stays the same. Not tough times, not good ones either. Despite today's annoyance, I'm grateful for change, trusting it will take me to new moments you have in mind.

By this shall all men know
that ye are my disciples,
if ye have love one to another.

John 13:35

Never let our need overshadow
our recognition of the needs of
others. Ground us in empathy.
Commission our sympathy. Urge
us to offer comforting hands and
understanding hearts. And in so
doing, show us how easing the
pain of others eases our own.

My soul thirsteth for God,
for the living God:
when shall I come and appear
before God?

Psalm 42:2

Comfort us, God, when we come
to this awesome conclusion:
What did not satisfy us when
we finally laid hold of it was
surely not the thing we were so
long in seeking. Yes, comfort us
by this recognition: In all our
longings, we are only yearning
for you.

Likewise the Spirit also helpeth
our infirmities: for we know not
what we should pray for as we ought:
but the Spirit itself maketh intercession
for us with groanings
which cannot be uttered.

Romans 8:26

When sorrow comes to us, it can be overwhelming. We feel unable to move and incapable of the patience necessary to wait for the healing that will come with time. Knowing you are there, Lord, brings the most comfort.

It is even harder to watch a loved one grieve. We feel left outside with no way to reach in and bring comfort. Words fail. Kind gestures fall short. But when we remember that what comforts us most is your presence, we know what to do: just be there—listening, praying, and loving— allowing your Spirit to pervade the space around us.

Be ye therefore perfect,
even as your Father
which is in heaven is perfect.

Matthew 5:48

O Lord, what a comfort it is to know that you are working to perfect us even on days when we feel anything but perfect. One day all creation will be perfected. How we look forward to that day when our faith is fully realized, and we are complete in you!

For as many as are led by the Spirit of God, they are the sons of God. For ye have not received the spirit of bondage again to fear; but ye have received the Spirit of adoption, whereby we cry, Abba, Father. The Spirit itself beareth witness with our spirit, that we are the children of God: And if children, then heirs; heirs of God, and joint-heirs with Christ; if so be that we suffer with him, that we may be also glorified together.

Romans 8:14–17

One sentiment I hear from time to time is "...after all, we're all God's children." It's usually uttered during trying times, to remind us to hold on and keep the faith. It's a comforting thought, but the passage here stresses that God's children are led by his Spirit. May we strive each day to be active children of God, praying and following the call of his Spirit rather than our own impulses and desires.

Now our Lord Jesus Christ himself,
and God, even our Father, which hath
loved us, and hath given us
everlasting consolation and good hope
through grace, comfort your hearts,
and stablish you in every good
word and work.

2 Thessalonians 2:16–17

Sometimes the circumstances of our lives are so difficult, Lord! Often misfortunes seem to come all at once. Other times ongoing, wear-me-down situations or relationships seem to follow us day in and day out. Then there are the crushing tragedies that strike us in our tracks and devastate us. A life of faith is not defined by these things—but it is not exempt, either. Suffering is as real for the faithful as for anyone else. Sometimes, it is difficult to trust. However, we have an "everlasting consolation and good hope" that lifts us up. In that comfort and hope, God carries us, heals us with the balm of his tender mercies, and strengthens us to carry on in what is good.

> Then shall thy light break forth
> as the morning, and thine health
> shall spring forth speedily:
> and thy righteousness shall go
> before thee; the glory of the Lord
> shall be thy reward.
>
> Isaiah 58:8

Dear Lord,

Someone I love is very sick and I am asking in prayer for a healing. I am afraid and anxious for this person and pray for a quick recovery to strength and wholeness again. I also seek guidance, Lord, in how I might best be able to help this person and be there for the support, comfort, and love they need most. I seek to be an angel and offer what I can and not be an extra burden to someone already dealing with stress and worry. Please wrap this person in your arms of love, security, and caring and be a beacon of light in a time of darkness so that they might not lose hope. Amen.

> And our hope of you is stedfast, knowing, that as ye are partakers of the sufferings, so shall ye be also of the consolation.
>
> 2 Corinthians 1:7

Dear Lord,

Today I received bad news about something I was so excited about, something I had poured my heart and soul into. I worked so hard on this project and to find out it just won't happen has all but broken my spirit. I ask for your comfort as I deal with this disappointment, and that you also help me to understand the bigger picture behind this. I know that your ways are mysterious, and that you never fail to open a new door when an old one closes, so keep my eyes and my heart focused on the future and the new doors this rejection may lead to. Lift my spirits with your love and faith in me and help me find my enthusiasm and belief in my own abilities again. Thank you, Lord.

> Mine eye also is dim by reason
> of sorrow, and all my members
> are as a shadow.

Job 17:7

Dear Lord,

My heart is broken today, for a dear friend has passed away. I'm lost in sorrow and the ache of knowing I'll never see my beloved friend again. My spirit is sad for her family and for all of those who knew and loved her, as I know their hearts are broken, too. I ask you in prayer for some comfort, for myself and for all those who are missing her and affected by her death. May your presence provide extra strength during such a tough time, and may your love soothe even the most shattered souls. Remind us that love truly never ceases, and that she will always be in our hearts and our minds. Amen.

And I will come down and talk with thee there: and I will take of the spirit which is upon thee, and will put it upon them; and they shall bear the burden of the people with thee, that thou bear it not thyself alone.

Numbers 11:17

God puts friends in our lives to comfort us, support us, and share our burdens during dark times. And groups of friends can be powerful, indeed: Carrie, a single mom of two who lost her consulting job during an economic downturn, still remembers the solace provided by the prayer circle at her community church as she interviewed for a new position. "I knew others were thinking of me and praying for me," she shares. "It gave me strength."

Dear Lord, in lonely and discouraging times, may I never lose sight of the people you have put in my life. May I always remember the power of loving kindness, multiplied!

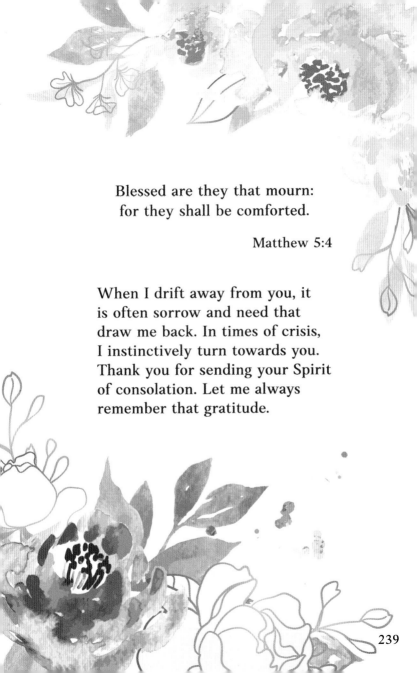

Blessed are they that mourn:
for they shall be comforted.

Matthew 5:4

When I drift away from you, it
is often sorrow and need that
draw me back. In times of crisis,
I instinctively turn towards you.
Thank you for sending your Spirit
of consolation. Let me always
remember that gratitude.

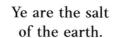

Ye are the salt
of the earth.

Matthew 5:13

Salt gives flavor and taste.
As Christians, we are called to
bring God's joy, love, and comfort
to others. Salt also preserves,
and we are also called to hold
to the truth against
corruption.

> In my Father's house are
> many mansions: if it were not so,
> I would have told you.
> I go to prepare a place for you.
>
> John 14:2

When I was a child, I imagined heaven to be an impersonal, abstract place, perhaps filled with fluffy white clouds, and harps, and singing angels. Somehow heaven lacked the comfort and warmth of my own bedroom, with its unique touches such as my favorite books and toys. Now that I am grown, I am no longer certain of what heaven will be like. Is it a "place" in the sense that I know: a field, or forest, or grassy knoll? Or is it unlike anything I have experienced in this lifetime? I cannot imagine, but heaven feels more personal to me when I remember the Biblical promise that there is a spot for me there—which the Lord has prepared! Now I wonder, what personal touches await? Lord, thank you for preparing an individual place for me in heaven.

Know therefore that the Lord thy God,
he is God, the faithful God,
which keepeth covenant and mercy
with them that love him
and keep his commandments
to a thousand generations.

Deuteronomy 7:9

Today I found out that a close friend has been diagnosed with pancreatic cancer. Dear God, this man was healthy. He kept fit and he ate a good diet. His family is devastated, and I am reminded of how quickly our lives can change. God, some change makes me afraid, and in the face of my fear, I must remember to have faith in you. I must never lose sight of the fact that you keep the faith for me, also; you are there for me. I can share my fears with you. I can unburden myself. I can ask you how to best support my friend and his loved ones. Dear God, please help me to remember that faith is a two-way street: even as I work to remain faithful to you and all you stand for, you are faithful to me, and I can take comfort in that fact.

Other refuge have I none;
Hangs my helpless soul on thee:
Leave, ah! leave me not alone,
Still support and comfort me.
All my trust on thee is stayed,
All my help from thee I bring;
Cover my defenseless head
with the shadow of thy wing!
Amen.

Traditional prayer

GOD'S FAITHFUL LOVE

He that loveth not knoweth not God;
for God is love.

1 John 4:8

> Cause me to hear thy lovingkindness
> in the morning; for in thee do I trust:
> cause me to know the way
> wherein I should walk; for I lift up
> my soul unto thee.
>
> Psalm 143:8

What a relief in this throwaway world of ever-changing values to know that you, O God, are the same yesterday, today, and tomorrow. Your trustworthiness and desire for all your children to have good things never varies. You are as sure as sunrise and sunset.

For God hath not given us the spirit of fear; but of power, and of love, and of a sound mind.

2 Timothy 1:7

We sometimes fear drawing close to God, who is the source of love. Yet, when we finally choose to draw near, what a wonderful discovery we make—we are loved completely.

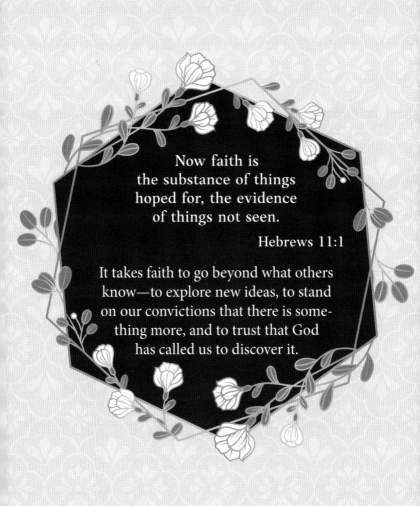

Now faith is
the substance of things
hoped for, the evidence
of things not seen.

Hebrews 11:1

It takes faith to go beyond what others
know—to explore new ideas, to stand
on our convictions that there is something more, and to trust that God
has called us to discover it.

Then saith he to Thomas,
Reach hither thy finger, and behold
my hands; and reach hither thy hand,
and thrust it into my side:
and be not faithless, but believing.
And Thomas answered and said
unto him, My Lord and my God.
Jesus saith unto him, Thomas,
because thou hast seen me,
thou hast believed: blessed are they
that have not seen,
and yet have believed.

John 20:27–29

Faith is knowing without seeing, believing without fully understanding, trusting without touching the One who is ever faithful.

Now he that planteth
and he that watereth are one:
and every man shall receive
his own reward according to
his own labour.

1 Corinthians 3:8

God shelters his people in the
short term and rewards them
in the long term. He uses his
strength as a refuge for those
who trust him.

Hear my prayer, O Lord, give ear to my supplications: in thy faithfulness answer me, and in thy righteousness.

Psalm 143:1

Lord, you have seen each time when I've been abandoned by those in whose love I have trusted. You have known the loneliness in my soul. I must confess to you that it causes me to wonder if your love has failed me, too. I need you to assure me that you are still here and that you will always stay with me.

Imagine, if you can...

A love so deep it swallows fear,

A love so wide it embraces pain,

A love so high it humbles pride,

A love so thick it absorbs all sin.

Imagine, but don't stop there!

Come with your fear,

Your pain,

Your pride,

Your sin.

Come to God who loves—

Purely, perfectly, precisely—

You.

Therefore we are buried with him by
baptism into death: that like as Christ
was raised up from the dead by
the glory of the Father, even so we
also should walk in newness of life.

Romans 6:4

No matter how deep a rut we dig
ourselves into, the arms of God are
long enough to lift us up into a newer
life free from struggle. No matter how
dark a tunnel we crawl into, the love
of God is strong enough to reach in
and guide us toward a brighter life,
free from fear.

But without faith it is impossible
to please him: for he that cometh
to God must believe that he is,
and that he is a rewarder of them
that diligently seek him.

Hebrews 11:6

Faith in a wise and trustworthy God, even
in broken times like these, teaches us a new
math: subtracting old ways and adding new
thoughts because sharing with God divides
our troubles and multiplies unfathomable
possibilities for renewed life.

From the dark night of the soul
comes the blessing of the dawn.
From the deep wounds of the heart
comes the gift of love reborn.
From the chaos of confusion
comes the calm of clarity.
From the anguish of discord
comes the peace of harmony.
From the grieving of great loss
comes the happiness of new life.
From the coldness of despair
comes the warmth of
our Father's light.

> For God so loved the world,
> that he gave his only begotten Son,
> that whosoever believeth
> in him should not perish,
> but have everlasting life.
>
> John 3:16

In this world where human love is conditional and often temporary, it is a joy to know that God loves us unconditionally and eternally. Nothing we can say or do will cause him to stop loving us. Our minds cannot even imagine the immensity of his love for each person on this planet. He sent his son to Earth to deliver that message of love personally. When he died for us, he was saying through his action, "I love you." God remains always ready to lavish his love on his children. May we open our hearts to receive all the love he has to offer.

That their hearts might be comforted,
being knit together in love,
and unto all riches of the full
assurance of understanding,
to the acknowledgement
of the mystery of God, and
of the Father, and of Christ;
In whom are hid all the treasures
of wisdom and knowledge.

Colossians 2:2–3

God, bless the unknown angels who clear the cluttered paths of the lost, who wipe the tears of the grieving, and who hold the hands that tremble in fear. Their names may be known only to you, but their acts of mercy give me the assurance and trust that your love touches everyone, everywhere. Amen.

You have the power, Lord, to heal me.
I don't doubt that for a minute.
You crafted me; you can re-create me.
I trust in your creative ability.
I know you love me.
You sent your beloved Son for my redemption
And you shower me with blessings daily.
I trust in your love, Lord,
Your desire to bring me health.
It's a little harder to trust in your wisdom.
I think I know what I want here.
I know what my healing will look like, sort of.
But how do you want to pull that off?
Seriously, what's your idea of my wholeness?
How would you like to accomplish my healing?
I'm guessing you'll want to touch
my mind, my soul,
My attitude, my relationships,
and—oh, yes—my health.
So let's do it, Lord.
I trust in your wisdom to heal all of me.
Amen.

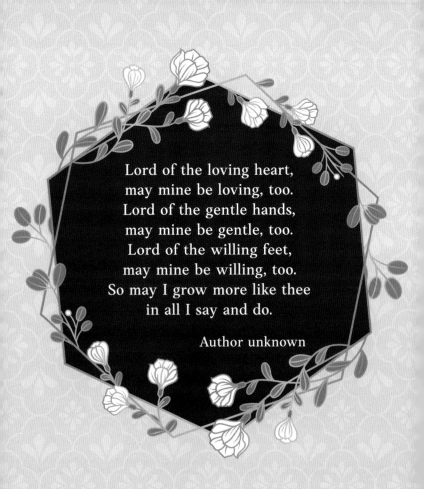

Lord of the loving heart,
may mine be loving, too.
Lord of the gentle hands,
may mine be gentle, too.
Lord of the willing feet,
may mine be willing, too.
So may I grow more like thee
in all I say and do.

Author unknown

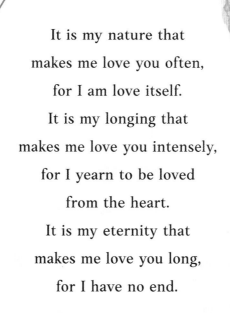

It is my nature that
makes me love you often,
for I am love itself.
It is my longing that
makes me love you intensely,
for I yearn to be loved
from the heart.
It is my eternity that
makes me love you long,
for I have no end.

Mechthild of Magdeburg

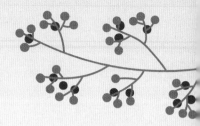

> I have blotted out, as a thick cloud,
> thy transgressions, and, as a cloud,
> thy sins: return unto me;
> for I have redeemed thee.
>
> Isaiah 44:22

O God, I am guilty of transgressions that make me ashamed, and I fear you'll leave me. Yet have you ever refused to forgive those who ask? Why would I be different? Reassured, I accept forgiveness and will share it with those who need it from me.

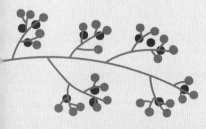

For he satisfieth
the longing soul,
and filleth the hungry soul
with goodness.

Psalm 107:9

None but God can
satisfy the longing
of the immortal soul;
as the heart was made
for him, he only can fill it.

Richard Trench

God loves each of us as
if there was only one of us.

St. Augustine

O Lord, your gift of love is often
distorted in this world of ours.
You are the source of the only
perfect love we will ever know.
Thank you, Lord, for abiding in us
and helping us love ourselves and
others. On this day, Lord, I pray
that you will draw near to anyone
who is feeling unloved. May they
accept your unconditional love so
they will know what true love is!

O Lord, thou art my God;
I will exalt thee, I will praise thy name;
for thou hast done wonderful things;
thy counsels of old are faithfulness
and truth.

Isaiah 25:1

Human faith lives between two extremes, Lord: It's neither completely blind nor able to see everything. It has plenty of evidence when it steps out and trusts you, but it takes each step with a good many questions still unanswered. It's really quite an adventure, this life of faith. And Lord, I must confess that experiencing your faithfulness over time makes it easier and easier to trust you with the unknown in life. Thank you for your unshakable devotion.

The Lord that delivered me out of the paw of the lion, and out of the paw of the bear, he will deliver me out of the hand of this Philistine.

1 Samuel 17:37

Lord, I know that it was not David's sling that won the victory against Goliath—it was David's trust in you. While David's older brothers and the other troops cowered in the camp because of Goliath's threats and taunts, David ran out to meet the giant in your name, Lord. It was you who gave that shepherd boy success. Oh, Lord! I want to be like David. I don't want to cower in fear, but to run out in faith in order to do your will.

> The sacrifices of God are a broken
> spirit: a broken and a contrite heart,
> O God, thou wilt not despise.
>
> Psalm 51:17

I am grateful that you don't require spiritual gymnastics from me when I sin, Lord. You just call me to come to you with a humble and repentant heart. In my pride I sometimes want to do something that will impress you—something that will "make up for it" somehow. But you just shake your head and keep calling me to humble myself and bring my sincere sorrow to you. That often doesn't seem like enough to me. But I guess that's the point: I can never earn your grace; it is a gift. Christ died on the cross for us because it is beyond our powers to make up for all the sins we have committed. I bring my contrite heart before you now, Lord. Thank you for receiving it as an acceptable sacrifice.

The Lord thy God in the midst of
thee is mighty; he will save,
he will rejoice over thee with joy;
he will rest in his love, he will joy
over thee with singing.

Zephaniah 3:17

Father, thank you for initiating our wonderful
relationship by loving me first! Your perfect
love has taught me to trust you and leave my
fear of your judgment behind. Your love for
me brings such joy to my life, Lord. Help me
spread this joy to others today.

He that trusteth in his riches
shall fall; but the righteous
shall flourish as a branch.

Proverbs 11:28

Lord, what comfort we find in your
changeless nature. When we look
back and remember all the ways
you've guided us in the past, we
know we have no need to be anxious
about the future. You were, are, and
always will be our Savior and Lord.
Why should we fear instability when
you are always here with us?

Thy mercy, O Lord, is in the heavens;
and thy faithfulness reacheth
unto the clouds.

Psalm 36:5

Lord, in my darkest moments, it is easy to despair and fear that you have given up on me. It would be understandable for you to be angry and disappointed and leave me to my ruin. How comforting it is to know that the minute I regret what I have done and turn to you, you are right where you have been all along—by my side, ready to embrace and carry me until I am strong enough to take a step on my own. Thank you for your faithfulness, Lord—especially when I least deserve it.

When Jesus saw their faith, he said unto the sick of the palsy, Son, thy sins be forgiven thee.

Mark 2:5

Imagine having the arms of a loving, caring angel wrapped around you when you are sad or upset. Faith is like that. Comforting and encouraging, faith is like a trustworthy old friend that is never too tired or busy to hear your problems or help you find your footing again when you stumble through life. Faith in God is our best friend and ally.

Now them that are such we command
and exhort by our Lord Jesus Christ,
that with quietness they work,
and eat their own bread.
But ye, brethren, be not weary
in well doing.

2 Thessalonians 3:12–13

Lord God, my feet are as sore as my spirit is
exhausted. Help me carry on in trust and do
the things I must each day for my family, my
community, and myself. Teach me to walk
even when it hurts and share the gifts you
have given me with the world.

Who is among you that feareth
the Lord, that obeyeth the voice of
his servant, that walketh
in darkness, and hath no light?
let him trust in the name of
the Lord, and stay upon his God.

Isaiah 50:10

O thou who art the Sun of
Righteousness and the Light
Eternal, giving gladness unto
all things; shine upon us both now
and for ever, that we may walk
always in the light of thy
countenance; through Jesus Christ
our Lord. Amen.

6th-century prayer

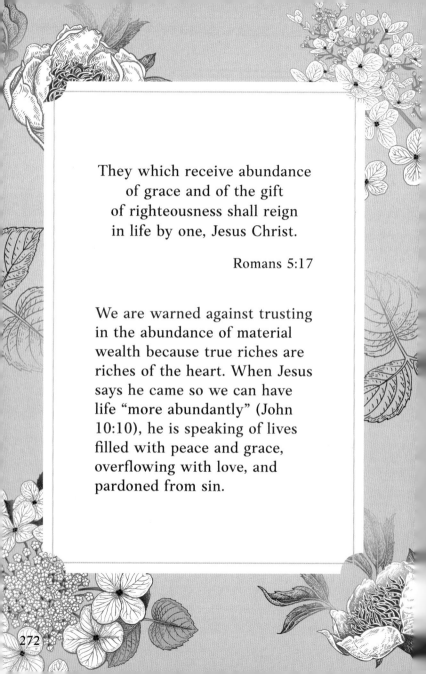

They which receive abundance
of grace and of the gift
of righteousness shall reign
in life by one, Jesus Christ.

Romans 5:17

We are warned against trusting
in the abundance of material
wealth because true riches are
riches of the heart. When Jesus
says he came so we can have
life "more abundantly" (John
10:10), he is speaking of lives
filled with peace and grace,
overflowing with love, and
pardoned from sin.

> The Lord also will be a refuge
> for the oppressed, a refuge in times
> of trouble. And they that know
> thy name will put their trust in thee:
> for thou, Lord, hast not forsaken them
> that seek thee.
>
> Psalm 9:9–10

The Lord is a refuge, a tower, a fortress, and a hiding place. All these terms are used in scripture to show that we are safe in him. He protects us and even hides us. This is a solace to our souls since our foes and fears are locked outside.

When pursued by doubt, perplexity, failure, or sorrow, we can know that "he shall hide me in his pavilion" (Psalm 27:5). It is David who often writes of this protection because David often needed it. David spent years hiding in caves, fleeing for his life from King Saul. He knows what he is writing about. And he knows the Lord does not forsake those who seek him.

One man of you shall chase a thousand:
for the Lord your God,
he it is that fighteth for you,
as he hath promised you.

Joshua 23:10

Sometimes we are exhausted from the battle.
But God fights for us. He may give us
extra strength for the battle, enough to
chase a thousand men. But ultimately, it is
his strength that prevails and his promise
that we trust. Whatever obstacles you face,
God is more than sufficient for your need,
entirely capable of renewing your spirit and
winning the day. He has promised you this.

The Lord hath appeared of old
unto me, saying, Yea, I have loved thee
with an everlasting love:
therefore with lovingkindness have
I drawn thee.

Jeremiah 31:3

God wants us to love him, not because
he is greedy for love, but because
when we are devoted to loving him,
we get in touch with his powerful,
everlasting love for us. When we do,
we cannot contain it, and it overflows
to others.

Hear, O Israel:
The Lord our God is one Lord:
And thou shalt love the Lord
thy God with all thine heart,
and with all thy soul,
and with all thy might.

Deuteronomy 6:4–5

God's desire for love from us is not primarily for his benefit, but for ours. One of his deepest desires is that we know his love, and somehow when we take action to love him, it is then we discover just how much he loves us.

> But we have this treasure
> in earthen vessels, that the excellency
> of the power may be of God,
> and not of us.
>
> 2 Corinthians 4:7

God, make me an open vessel through which the waters of your Spirit flow freely. Let your love move through me and out into my world, touching everyone I come in contact with. Express your joy through the special talents you have given me, that others may come to know your presence in their own lives by witnessing your presence in mine. Amen.

The Lord recompense thy work,
and a full reward be given thee
of the Lord God of Israel,
under whose wings
thou art come to trust.

Ruth 2:12

Thank you, Lord, for reaching
out and drawing me under your
wings. Even though I am just one
of billions of people who need
you, your love is so great that you
know my troubles, are concerned
for my welfare, and are working to
renew my dreams. I am so blessed
to have you to turn to when I am
faced with a calamity, and I am
so very grateful that I have you to
lean on. I praise you with all my
heart. Amen.

And beside this, giving all diligence,
add to your faith virtue; and to
virtue knowledge; And to knowledge
temperance; and to temperance
patience; and to patience godliness;
And to godliness brotherly kindness;
and to brotherly kindness charity.
For if these things be in you,
and abound, they make you that
ye shall neither be barren
nor unfruitful in the knowledge of
our Lord Jesus Christ.

2 Peter 1:5–8

Among the proliferation of bumper-sticker slogans, statements, and sentiments, there's one sticker that encourages people to "practice random acts of kindness." It's a great little reminder. For whenever we make a conscious effort to be kind to others —especially to those whom we usually tend to avoid, overlook, or ignore—we take the first step toward seeing them as God sees them: through the eyes of love.

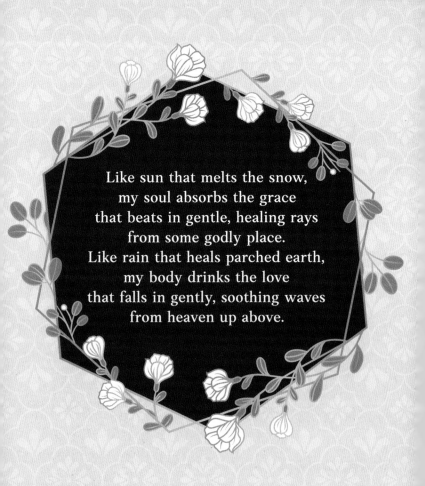

Like sun that melts the snow,
my soul absorbs the grace
that beats in gentle, healing rays
from some godly place.
Like rain that heals parched earth,
my body drinks the love
that falls in gently, soothing waves
from heaven up above.

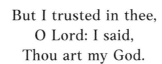

But I trusted in thee,
O Lord: I said,
Thou art my God.

Psalm 31:14

Dear Lord, when I am sad, you give me hope. When I am lost, you offer me direction and guidance. When I am alone, you stand beside me. When my heart aches with sorrow, you bring me new blessings. Thank you for your gifts of grace, of love, and of healing. Amen.

But after that the kindness and love of God our Saviour toward man appeared, Not by works of righteousness which we have done, but according to his mercy he saved us, by the washing of regeneration, and renewing of the Holy Ghost.

Titus 3:4–5

Dear God, complaints sometimes come first before I can feel free to love you. Sometimes you seem distant and unreasonable, even uncaring. Help me understand why life can be so hurtful and hard. Hear my complaints and, in the spirit of compassion, show me how to move through pain to rebirth, trusting in you.

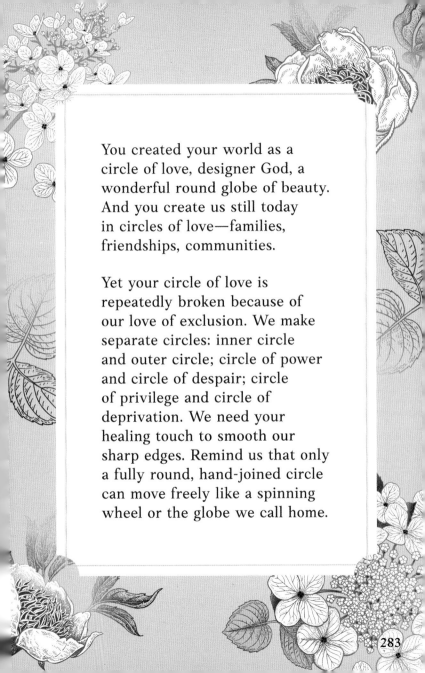

You created your world as a
circle of love, designer God, a
wonderful round globe of beauty.
And you create us still today
in circles of love—families,
friendships, communities.

Yet your circle of love is
repeatedly broken because of
our love of exclusion. We make
separate circles: inner circle
and outer circle; circle of power
and circle of despair; circle
of privilege and circle of
deprivation. We need your
healing touch to smooth our
sharp edges. Remind us that only
a fully round, hand-joined circle
can move freely like a spinning
wheel or the globe we call home.

As the Father hath loved me, so have
I loved you: continue ye in my love.

John 15:9

Love. It seems so simple. Love is a gift
given. Yet, if we don't overlook it, Lord,
we treat it like a gift certificate saved
so long it expires. We are down-on-
our-knees grateful your gifts of love
and grace never expire. Nudge us to use
them, for we lose their value each day
they go unclaimed. We stay disconnected
from you, the source of creation and
re-creation. To connect only requires
a "Yes!" from us. Hear us shout!

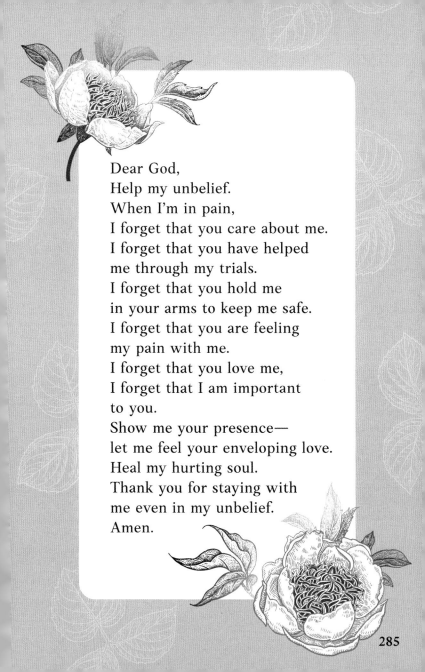

Dear God,
Help my unbelief.
When I'm in pain,
I forget that you care about me.
I forget that you have helped
me through my trials.
I forget that you hold me
in your arms to keep me safe.
I forget that you are feeling
my pain with me.
I forget that you love me,
I forget that I am important
to you.
Show me your presence—
let me feel your enveloping love.
Heal my hurting soul.
Thank you for staying with
me even in my unbelief.
Amen.

> I do set my bow in the cloud,
> and it shall be for a token of
> a covenant between me and the earth.
>
> Genesis 9:13

God gave the rainbow as a sign of his promise to never flood the entire earth again. The colors that spread out in spectrum, as sunlight passes through water droplets in the sky, speak of God's faithfulness in keeping his promise to Noah and to all the generations that have followed. Faithfulness marks God's character. It is who he is, through and through. Let every rainbow we see remind us of God's faithful love, and let praise flow from our hearts to the one who always keeps his promises.

But whoso hath this world's good,
and seeth his brother have need,
and shutteth up his bowels
of compassion from him,
how dwelleth the love of God
in him?

1 John 3:17

Lord, give me your compassion
today. When I look at the people
around me, help me to see them
through your eyes. I know you love
us all equally, Lord. And you love
us completely and unconditionally.
May I compassionately reach out
to others in your name today.

Howbeit when he, the Spirit of truth,
is come, he will guide you into
all truth: for he shall not speak
of himself; but whatsoever
he shall hear, that shall he speak:
and he will shew you things to come.

John 16:13

Father, you're always calling to us to
turn our backs on sin and turn our
faces toward you. You even promise
to give us your own Spirit to lead and
guide us and strengthen us to walk in
your ways. I praise you today for your
tireless love and concern for all
people and for reaching out
to us with your message
of salvation.

> Then Peter said unto them, Repent,
> and be baptized every one of you in
> the name of Jesus Christ
> for the remission of sins, and ye shall
> receive the gift of the Holy Ghost.
> For the promise is unto you,
> and to your children, and to all that
> are afar off, even as many as the Lord
> our God shall call.
>
> Acts 2:38–39

Lord, how we love to contemplate your sojourn on Earth. How you came that we might see heaven in your eyes even as the earth was beneath your feet. How you were present in the lives of those who walked with you and attentive to the unspoken needs of every heart. How we love to tell of your sacrifice on the cross so that all of us might one day share eternal life with you. It's the story that never grows old, the only story that has the power to save, the power to transform hearts.

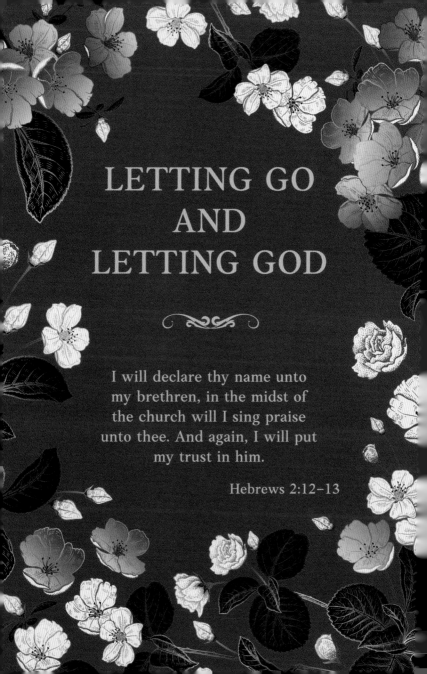

LETTING GO AND LETTING GOD

I will declare thy name unto
my brethren, in the midst of
the church will I sing praise
unto thee. And again, I will put
my trust in him.

Hebrews 2:12–13

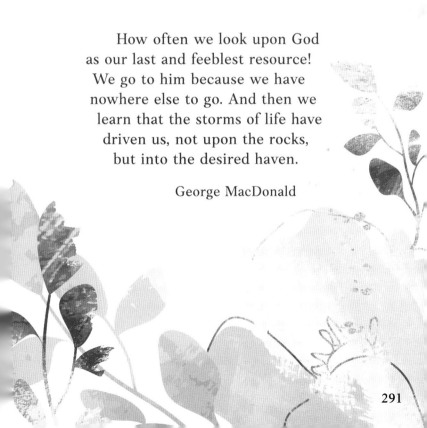

And they came to him,
and awoke him,
saying, Master, master, we perish.
Then he arose, and rebuked the wind
and the raging of the water:
and they ceased, and there was a calm.

Luke 8:24

How often we look upon God
as our last and feeblest resource!
We go to him because we have
nowhere else to go. And then we
learn that the storms of life have
driven us, not upon the rocks,
but into the desired haven.

George MacDonald

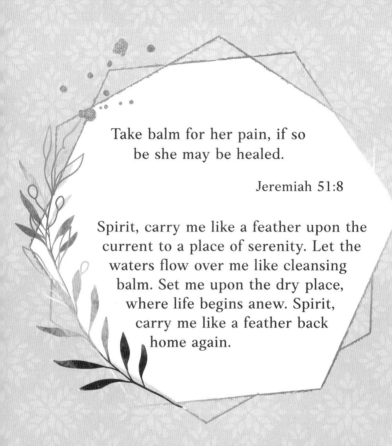

Take balm for her pain, if so
be she may be healed.

Jeremiah 51:8

Spirit, carry me like a feather upon the
current to a place of serenity. Let the
waters flow over me like cleansing
balm. Set me upon the dry place,
where life begins anew. Spirit,
carry me like a feather back
home again.

> But go ye and learn what
> that meaneth, I will have mercy,
> and not sacrifice: for I am not come
> to call the righteous,
> but sinners to repentance.
>
> Matthew 9:13

God knows that as hard as we may try, there are times when we will make human mistakes. Even so, if we trust in him and ask his forgiveness, he will bless us with mercy and peace. We just need to let go of our pride and shame, and let God love us.

For he is our peace, who hath made both one, and hath broken down the middle wall of partition between us.

Ephesians 2:14

Peace describes the state of being we all desire to have. The word "peace" brings to mind "the absence of war." It evokes images of people getting along with one another and living together in harmony. A similar sense comes from having inner peace: a quality of internal rest and calm. But neither kind of peace can be had without paying the price for it: We must release everything to God. We know that we've acquired true peace if, when things are chaotic all around us, we can be calm and trust in the One of whom the Bible says, "He is our peace..."

The righteous shall be
glad in the Lord, and shall
trust in him; and all the upright
in heart shall glory.

Psalm 64:10

We all make plans for our lives and
have an agenda we want to hold on
to. Yet if we let go and let God be
in charge, the result will
bring us peace.

> If ye then, being evil, know how to give good gifts unto your children, how much more shall your Father which is in heaven give good things to them that ask him?
>
> Matthew 7:11

If I count the things I've asked for that you have not given me, I begin to believe you do not love me, God. But if, instead, I bring to mind all of the goodness you have shown me, I come to trust that you have never given me less than what I need and often have blessed me with far more from a depth of love I cannot comprehend.

The fruit of righteousness is
sown in peace of them
that make peace.

James 3:18

Oh Lord, I do not know how to
deal with this person. I am afraid
and angry, and my heart aches
with sadness. I turn to you, God,
and ask for the peace that passes
all understanding. I surrender the
yoke of my burden to you, that
your will be done, not mine. Let
me rest in the healing waters of
your ever-present Spirit, now and
forever. Amen.

> Take my yoke upon you, and learn of me; for I am meek and lowly in heart: and ye shall find rest unto your souls.
>
> Matthew 11:29

When the nights seem long, the days feel like a struggle, and the spirit is weary, we find a resting place in God's enduring love, and we know that his plan for us is good. This is the true meaning of letting go and letting God's higher will be done in our lives.

Bless the Lord,
ye his angels, that
excel in strength, that do his
commandments, hearkening unto
the voice of his word.

Psalm 103:20

We are often harsh because we are
afraid—afraid of being hurt. We can
take a lesson from the angels who
trust their creator and do not
fear; they can touch their
charges with a
gentle hand.

You are the mighty wind
that lifts me up on high
when I am weak and weary
and without the strength to fly.
You are the mighty fortress
that keeps me free from fear
and shelters me in kindness
with your tender, loving care.

> For this cause also thank we God
> without ceasing, because,
> when ye received the word of God
> which ye heard of us, ye received it
> not as the word of men,
> but as it is in truth, the word of God,
> which effectually worketh also in you
> that believe.
>
> 1 Thessalonians 2:13

God, sometimes I wish I could be saved from the struggle and pain of learning the hard way. But, Lord, that's not your plan, and I need to be willing to wait as you work gently from the inside out. Please grant me some strength in this time of uncertainty. I trust and love you. Amen.

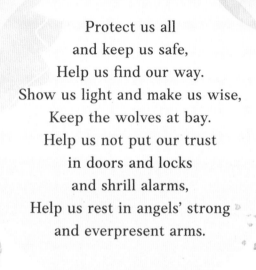

Protect us all
and keep us safe,
Help us find our way.
Show us light and make us wise,
Keep the wolves at bay.
Help us not put our trust
in doors and locks
and shrill alarms,
Help us rest in angels' strong
and everpresent arms.

In your patience possess ye your souls.

Luke 21:19

Be patient with everyone, but above all with yourself...do not be disheartened by your imperfections, but always rise up with fresh courage. How are we to be patient in dealing with our neighbor's faults if we are impatient in dealing with our own?

St. Francis de Sales

They that trust in their wealth,
and boast themselves in
the multitude of their riches;
None of them can by any means
redeem his brother, nor give
to God a ransom for him.

Psalm 49:6–7

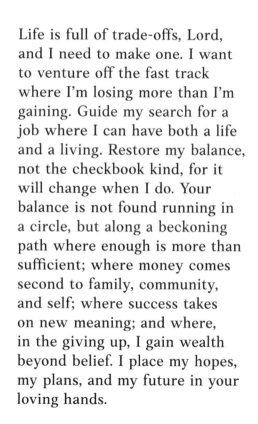

Life is full of trade-offs, Lord, and I need to make one. I want to venture off the fast track where I'm losing more than I'm gaining. Guide my search for a job where I can have both a life and a living. Restore my balance, not the checkbook kind, for it will change when I do. Your balance is not found running in a circle, but along a beckoning path where enough is more than sufficient; where money comes second to family, community, and self; where success takes on new meaning; and where, in the giving up, I gain wealth beyond belief. I place my hopes, my plans, and my future in your loving hands.

> Stand fast therefore in the liberty
> wherewith Christ hath made us free,
> and be not entangled again with the
> yoke of bondage.
>
> Galatians 5:1

Tossing leaves onto a fire, we name
them as regrets and failures from which
we choose to be free. We trust you to
redeem even these, our deadest moments.
They, like autumn leaves, can make the
brightest blaze.

Stir new possibilities into life from the
embers; fan the sparks of dreams so that
we may become one with your purpose
for us. It is the root from which we, leaf
and human life, begin and from which the
most amazing new creation can burst into
being, a flame in the darkness.

I know that faith is
what keeps me moving forward.
But sometimes, too,
my trust allows a leisure like this.
For you, God, are the one
who upholds all things.
Even as I sit here in stillness,
your breath keeps me breathing,
your mind keeps me thinking,
your love keeps me
yearning for home.

> Except the Lord build the house,
> they labour in vain that build it:
> except the Lord keep the city,
> the watchman waketh but in vain.
>
> Psalm 127:1

Sometimes I try to do too much "building" and "guarding" by my own efforts, Father. Thank you for the reminder that everything I do to further my own cause and ensure my own safety isn't going to be effective apart from an abiding trust in you. Help me remember, too, that you aren't just an element of my life, like some add-on magic charm to hedge all my bets. Forgive me for the times I've treated you like that! You're no optional feature. You are my provision and my protection—you are my very life. Thank you for the peace of mind that always comes when I stop trying to do it myself and tap into your unending supply of strength.

And whatsoever ye do, do it heartily, as to the Lord, and not unto men.

Colossians 3:23

I have always liked the expression, "You aren't the boss of me!" I'm an independent person, I run my own business, and I like being in control. And yet, sometimes I need to be reminded that there is someone I'm answerable to, and that someone is God. God asks that I be accountable in my actions, in the choices I make, and in the example I set for others, at home and in the world. I try to live my life with abandon, and when I keep God's Word first and foremost in my thinking, I find I can live fully in a way that feels good. God, you are my ultimate boss and I thank you!

My righteousness is near;
my salvation is gone forth,
and mine arms shall judge the people;
the isles shall wait upon me,
and on mine arm shall they trust.

Isaiah 51:5

Sometimes, God, I get too persnickety
and alarmingly tidy. I suppose I think
it's a way I can control my life. When
that happens, shake me up like a snow
globe so I can be real. Truly, messily,
and welcomingly real.

I have lost some of my zeal to do the work here, God. Forgive me for falling into despair and for being on the lookout for a greener pasture at the expense of full concentration on the tasks at hand. Help me not to cheat my employer by only giving a half-hearted effort.

But most of all, I want to keep my eyes on you, Lord, not on things or places or the myriad circumstances beyond my control. I know that true happiness and fulfillment will come only from being in your will.

And when it is time to move, you will show me. Therefore, strengthen my faith in your goodness. For I know your commitment to me has never been in question. Your zeal for my life never cools. Praise you!

> Mary kept all these things,
> and pondered them in her heart.
>
> Luke 2:19

Mary delighted in her son. What an honor it was to have such an intimate connection to Jesus. And what a wonderful, loving mother Mary was! As she listened to the amazing things the visiting shepherds had to say about her precious child, Mary quietly listened, pondering these things and filing them away in her heart. May all mothers look to Mary's example, Lord. May we parent generously and wisely, gently encouraging our children to look to your plans for their lives. Please help me let go, trusting that you will be their loving parent at all times.

But we all, with open face beholding
as in a glass the glory of the Lord,
are changed into the same image
from glory to glory,
even as by the Spirit of the Lord.

2 Corinthians 3:18

Dear God, I long to change parts of my life that are no longer working, but don't know where to start. Help me break down these big, scary goals into small and achievable steps. Give me courage to put these plans into action and turn my life around!

It is better to trust
in the Lord than to put
confidence in princes.

Psalm 118:9

I know with God on my side, I cannot
fail. Together, we make joyful plans
that are infused with his love and
grace. All I do is listen for his
voice within and I am on my
way to a bold, new me!

And Mary said,
My soul doth magnify the Lord,
And my spirit hath rejoiced
in God my Saviour.

Luke 1:46–47

Jesus, let me open my heart to you as your mother did. Mary didn't know what would happen, but she chose to follow God's plan. What an amazing woman of faith! I see echoes of her faith in some of the people I know from church, wise men and women who have a sense of inner peace about them. I know I want to be like that: let me start by saying yes to your plan for me today.

The Lord is not slack
concerning his promise,
as some men count slackness;
but is longsuffering to us-ward,
not willing that any should perish,
but that all should come
to repentance.

2 Peter 3:9

The promise here is Christ's promise to
return. We want him to return and set
things right. So much is messed up and we
long for him to come and rule with justice
and mercy. Justice and mercy, though, are
already part of his character and his plan.
Especially mercy. His very delay is so that
no one would perish, and that all should
repent. This is his mercy. So, while we
wait, remember his promise is true. He just
wants more people to take advantage of it.

> Blessed be the God and Father of
> our Lord Jesus Christ, who hath
> blessed us with all spiritual blessings
> in heavenly places in Christ.
>
> Ephesians 1:3

May the blessing of God fill your days.
Especially, may you develop the perfect
balance between duties to family and
responsibilities at work and worship.
As you seek serenity in these things,
may you find great cause for celebration,
knowing that the one who loves you
unconditionally remains at the center of
all your activity.

The God who hung the stars
in space will turn
your darkness into light.
The God whose birds rise
on the winds will give
your injured soul new flight.
The God who taught the whale
its song will cause
your heart to sing again.
For the God whose power
made Earth and sky
will touch you with
his gentle hand.

And the Lord shall guide thee continually,
and satisfy thy soul in drought,
and make fat thy bones: and thou shalt be
like a watered garden, and like
a spring of water, whose waters fail not.

Isaiah 58:11

Help me be open to your guidance,
Lord, however it comes. When
you speak to me in the words of
a friend, open my ears. When you
touch me in the embrace of a family
member, let me feel your gentle
touch. And when you come to me
in the almost imperceptible rush
of angels' wings, alert my
senses to your presence.

And he said, Go forth, and stand
upon the mount before the Lord.
And, behold, the Lord passed by, and
a great and strong wind rent
the mountains, and brake in pieces
the rocks before the Lord;
but the Lord was not in the wind:
and after the wind an earthquake; but
the Lord was not in the earthquake:
And after the earthquake a fire;
but the Lord was not in the fire:
and after the fire a still small voice.

1 Kings 19:11–12

Lord, you come to us in the storm, the fire,
and most of all the stillness of a quiet
moment. Sometimes your message is strong,
carried on bustling angelic wings; sometimes our spirits are nudged, our hearts
lightened by the gentle whisper of spirit
voices. However you approach us, your
message is always one of tender love and
compassion. Thank you for the certainty
—and the surprise—of your holy voice.

And walk in love, as Christ also hath loved us, and hath given himself for us an offering and a sacrifice to God for a sweetsmelling savour.

Ephesians 5:2

The people I know who walk in the ways of God are savory with the fruit of God's Spirit; they're the kind of people I can't be around enough. Their kind and gentle ways radiate peace. Their joy is contagious. Their faithfulness is inspiring. So many things about them make me want to be more like them—and more like Christ.

Think-
est thou that
I cannot now pray
to my Father, and he
shall presently give me more
than twelve legions of angels?

Matthew 26:53

Heavenly Father, your son, Jesus,
could have called down heaven to
destroy his enemies when he was on
Earth, but he didn't. Revenge wasn't
his mission. Love was. Help me
to submit, as he did, to a path
of gentleness in
the strength
of your love.
Amen.

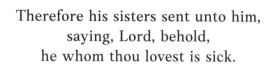

Therefore his sisters sent unto him,
saying, Lord, behold,
he whom thou lovest is sick.

John 11:3

I move through my days with a
sense of purpose, but sometimes I
am so consumed by the immediate
to-dos that I forget to be open to—
or even aware of—opportunities
for compassion. This week was no
exception. My mind has been on a
tight work deadline, and at night,
I've been tackling a series of home
repairs. It was only when my spouse
sat me down and made me put my
phone aside that I slowed down long
enough to learn that a close friend
of ours has been battling depression.
If I'd been paying attention, I might
have seen the signals. "Why don't
you give him a call?" was my
spouse's gentle suggestion. God,
help me to be sensitive to those I
love, and those in need. Jesus was
responsive when he learned that
Lazarus was sick; may I likewise
show compassion.

> He healeth the broken in heart,
> and bindeth up their wounds.
>
> Psalm 147:3

When someone breaks our heart, we mourn, we grieve, and we feel the pain of rejection. We pray to God for healing and relief. And then we pick up the pieces and, with God's help and guidance, rebuild a heart that is even stronger, more resilient, and ready to love again.

Brethren, be not children
in understanding:
howbeit in malice be ye children,
but in understanding be men.

1 Corinthians 14:20

God, I give thanks for the wisdom you share with me when I am trying to understand my own actions or someone else's. You know what is best, and you have my highest good in mind. I will turn to you for the advice and guidance I need, and let go of my own need for control. Thank you, God, for being a strong and loving presence in my life. Amen.

Yea, before the day was I am he;
and there is none that can deliver
out of my hand: I will work,
and who shall let it?

Isaiah 43:13

When teetering here on the "cutting edge" of technology, cyberspace, and everything in between, O God, it is reassuring to know that from the beginning of time, you guide, direct, and hear our voices as we continue to ask for guidance.

> If any man serve me, let him follow me; and where I am, there shall also my servant be: if any man serve me, him will my Father honour.
>
> John 12:26

Heavenly Father, just for today, please keep my eyes open, my hands willing, and my heart eager to help everyone in need who crosses my path, even if the need is as small as an encouraging smile, even if the need requires a sacrifice of time and talent. Just for today, God. With your guidance, I have faith that, day by day, I can help more and give more.

And be not conformed
to this world: but be ye
transformed by the renewing
of your mind, that ye may prove
what is that good,
and acceptable, and perfect,
will of God.

Romans 12:2

My God is an awesome God,
for he not only loves me, he
empowers me to strive to be the
best I can be every day. I am
always provided with new
opportunities to shine, as long
as I hold fast to my faith in him,
and listen for his guidance.

Commit thy way unto the Lord;
trust also in him;
and he shall bring it to pass.

Psalm 37:5

Guidance is there, but you must look
with your heart. Let go of what
the mind and ego see, for it is
not the truth. Follow where your
heart leads, for it is led by the
spirit of a loving and powerful God
who wants what is best for you!

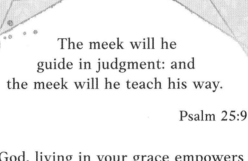

The meek will he
guide in judgment: and
the meek will he teach his way.

Psalm 25:9

God, living in your grace empowers me
to be the person I was born to be! I
look and listen for your guidance,
and I move with gratitude in the
direction that will help me
achieve the great things
you expect of me.

The entrance of thy words giveth light;
it giveth understanding unto the simple.

Psalm 119:130

Psalm 119 focuses on the blessing of scripture, describing it as "a lamp unto my feet, and a light unto my path" (verse 105). It is no small thing, this promise that scripture will give "understanding unto the simple." It will give understanding to the wise as well, bringing to light the motives of men and the mercies of God.

Illumination and guidance are promised to those who study it and meditate on it. The Apostle James likens it to a mirror in which we truly see ourselves (James 1:22–25). But it is also the word by which God "hath shined in our hearts, to give the light of the knowledge of the glory of God" (2 Corinthians 4:6).

> But they that wait upon the Lord shall renew their strength; they shall mount up with wings as eagles; they shall run, and not be weary; and they shall walk, and not faint.
>
> Isaiah 40:31

Lord, your word created all there is. Let it now create a powerful restoration within me. Your love sustains all life. Let it now sustain and renew me. Your strength holds up the galaxies. Let it now hold me up and give me support. Your light reaches the far ends of the universe. Let it shine its healing energy upon me now. Amen.

And it came to pass in those days,
that he went out into a mountain
to pray, and continued all night
in prayer to God.

Luke 6:12

O God, my days are frantic dashes between
have to, ought, and should. There is no
listening bone in me. Lead me to a porch
step or a swing, a chair or a hillside, where
I can be restored by sitting, Lord, simply
sitting. With you there to meet me, sitting
places become prime places for collecting
thoughts, not to mention fragmented lives.

And God said, Let there be lights
in the firmament of the heaven
to divide the day from the night;
and let them be for signs, and for
seasons, and for days, and years.

Genesis 1:14

We can relax, O Lord of light,
during the long dark nights of
winter, knowing that in order
for trees to blossom and bear
fruit and the maple tree to yield
its sugar, a resting stillness of
dormancy is a welcome part
of growth.

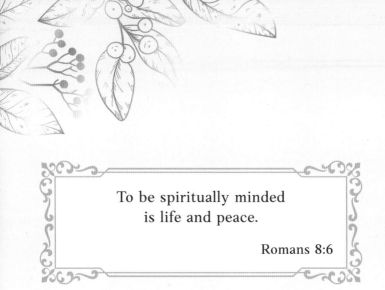

> To be spiritually minded
> is life and peace.
>
> Romans 8:6

Today I feel alone, yet I am not lonely. There is peace in solitude and rejuvenation in the quiet of being alone. Lead my thoughts to restful healing, Lord. Help me use this time alone to find myself and reach deep inside my heart and mind to find peace. I rejoice in being away from the noise and clatter of everyday life and praise God for letting me have this time for myself.

But let us, who are of the day,
be sober, putting on the breastplate
of faith and love; and for an helmet,
the hope of salvation.

1 Thessalonians 5:8

God,
I am feeling tired and weary and
weak. I do my best each day, and
often it just doesn't seem good
enough. I lose hope and enthusiasm
and a sense of purpose to carry on.
I pray today for restored hope in my
heart, and a new vision of possibility
in my soul. I pray you will assure
me of better days to come, and
that in the meantime, I am never
alone in my struggles. I pray for a
rejuvenated body with energy to
continue to pursue my passions and
dreams. Give me hope again, God,
because my life is not over yet. Take
my hand and pull me up so that I
can get on my feet again and keep
moving forward into the future.
Amen.

For we are saved by hope:
but hope that is seen is not hope:
for what a man seeth, why doth
he yet hope for? But if we hope
for that we see not, then do we
with patience wait for it.

Romans 8:24–25

To have hope is to put our life
into the hands of a loving God
that is always looking out for us,
always making clear our path.
When we are feeling down and
about to give up, hope is like the
sign on the road that tells us "rest
stop ahead," and suddenly we feel
renewed and refreshed, able to
walk on just a bit longer and just
a bit farther than we thought we
could alone.

> Ye shall seek me, and find me,
> when ye shall search for me
> with all your heart.
>
> Jeremiah 29:13

Father, I thank you for the spiritual restlessness that drives me to seek a deeper relationship with you. Sometimes I try to fill what I perceive as gaps in my life with other things—work, hobbies, social media. I shy away from feeling incomplete. Let me fill my life with those gifts that are from you, God, and let me continue to seek you instead of settling for substitutes that seem to nourish or entertain for a while but ultimately do not satisfy.

PRAISE AND THANKSGIVING

And he hath put a new song
in my mouth, even praise unto
our God: many shall see it, and fear,
and shall trust in the Lord.

Psalm 40:3

Godliness with
contentment is
great gain.

1 Timothy 6:6

I celebrate the gift of
contentment, knowing
there is no guarantee it
will last. But for now,
it's great to rest—just
rest—in this wonderful,
trusting calm. Thank
you, Lord.

After making plans to go hiking with friends, I remembered my boots were a half size too small. My budget, however, was telling me that new footwear was out of the question. Without much hope, I decided to visit a sporting-goods store. As I drove there, I spotted a thrift store and felt a strong impulse to stop in. "God, please let there be a good pair of hiking boots in my size here," I prayed. Scanning the rows of shoes, I found only one pair of authentic hiking boots, and they were in new condition. But would they fit? I fumbled to find the sizing information. When I read it, I wanted to let out a whoop, but instead I whispered, "Thank you, God!" Then, handing the cashier a mere eight dollars and some change, I couldn't help but say "Thank you" again.

> I will speak of
> the glorious honour of thy majesty,
> and of thy wondrous works.
>
> Psalm 145:5

Every moment we are alive is full of reasons to sing out in joyful gratitude. Every breath we are given is a reminder that the glory of life is at hand. In the people we love, in the beauty of nature, in the golden sun that rises each morning—miracles are everywhere.

Then those men, when they had seen
the miracle that Jesus did, said,
This is of a truth that prophet that
should come
into the world.

John 6:14

Thank you, Lord, for your
miracles large and small: the
friend we meet by "coinci-
dence" when one of us needs
to hear an uplifting word, the
car accident averted just in
time, the healing of ills.

> Give thanks unto the Lord,
> call upon his name, make known
> his deeds among the people.
>
> 1 Chronicles 16:8

Heavenly Father, we are thankful for family.
Please bring our family together in happiness.
Help us see everything as your children do:
with wonder and awe. Glorious are your
creations! Thank you for creating us. We love
our family. We love you. Amen.

> O taste and see that the Lord is good:
> blessed is the man
> that trusteth in him.
>
> Psalm 34:8

Forgive me for complaining, dear God. Help me to remember that every time I have a headache, someone I know may have a hidden heartache; every time I don't like the food, millions have nothing to eat; every time I think my paycheck is small, too many people have no paycheck at all; every time I wish my loved ones were not so demanding, some people have no one to love. When I look around at my blessings, my complaints seem little. Teach me perspective, God, and to be grateful for my everyday gifts of family, food, and home. Let me always remember that you are good. Amen.

The day is thine,
the night also is thine:
thou hast prepared
the light and the sun.

Psalm 74:16

Praised be my Lord and God,
with all his creatures, and
especially our brother the
sun, who brings us the day
and brings us the light; fair is
he, and he shines with great
splendor. O Lord, he is a sign
to us of you! Praised be my
Lord for our sister the moon,
and for stars, set clear and
lovely in the heaven.

St. Francis of Assisi

Our fathers trusted in thee:
they trusted,
and thou didst deliver them.

Psalm 22:4

Thank you for the gift of ancestral faith.
May I, as I take my place in the family
portrait as the next generation, continue
to keep you, everlasting God, as the
centerpiece of our family, for your love is
as ageless and steadfast as the wind calling
my name. Watch over the grandchildren
as you have over me in your special ways.
Listen as I call out their names in echoes of
those family prayers shared on my behalf
through a lifetime of faith-full love.

Rejoice evermore.
Pray without ceasing.
In every thing give thanks:
for this is the will of God
in Christ Jesus concerning you.

1 Thessalonians 5:16–18

We accept your invitation to pray
without ceasing. Hear us as we
pray boldly, with expectation,
trusting your assurance that we
deserve to be in your presence
and to talk all we want. We are
grateful that you welcome us at all
times and in all places and moods.

> My voice shalt thou hear
> in the morning, O Lord;
> in the morning will I direct my prayer
> unto thee, and will look up.
>
> Psalm 5:3

God, you are so great. It is always the right time to worship you, but morning is best. Praise for the dawning light that streams in through this window. Praise for the sound of the birds as they flit through the air. Praise for the little spider crawling along on the ceiling. Praise for the smell of coffee and the warmth of a cup in my hands. Praise for the flowering plants—and even those weeds growing by the house. Praise for the neighbors walking along the sidewalk and the clouds moving by, too. Most of all, praise for the breath that keeps flowing in and out of my lungs. Yes, this is the greatest item of praise: that you alone are my life—all life itself. Without you, all is dust. Praise you!

Praise ye the Lord.
Praise God in his sanctuary:
praise him in the firmament
of his power. Praise him
for his mighty acts:
praise him according
to his excellent greatness.

Psalm 150:1–2

Let us therefore desire nothing
else, wish for nothing else,
and let nothing please and delight
us except our Creator
and Redeemer, and Savior.

St. Francis of Assisi

Take heed therefore unto yourselves,
and to all the flock, over the which
the Holy Ghost hath made you overseers,
to feed the church of God, which he hath
purchased with his own blood.

Acts 20:28

Lord, today my heart is full of gratitude
for your church. Thank you for asking
us to meet together to honor you. What
power there is in voicing our thanks
and petitions together! What
comfort in the outstretched arms
of friends! Protect us, Lord. Keep
us strong in faith, trust, hope, and
love—now and in the days to come.

> For we brought nothing into
> this world, and it is certain
> we can carry nothing out.
> And having food and raiment
> let us be therewith content.
>
> 1 Timothy 6:7–8

Content with just food and clothing?
Really, Lord? I'm thankful that you provide
for my basic needs, but there's much, much
more on my wish list. This passage makes
me realize how much I expect in life.
Sometimes I act like I'm entitled to certain
things: a well-paying job for little effort on
my part, minimal traffic on the way to said
job, restaurant lunches every day, seamless
relationships with loved ones. Help me
to be thankful for the countless blessings
in my life and to always be ready to help
others rather than focusing on adding to
my own stores. Please guide me, Lord. I'm
ready to answer your call to contentment.

And the apostles said
unto the Lord,
Increase our faith.

Luke 17:5

Lord, today I want to praise
you for giving me the faith
to believe and trust, for
faith itself is a gift from
you. I lift up to you today all
those I know who are having
trouble accepting your gift of
salvation. Be patient with
them, Lord. Reveal yourself
to them in a way that will
reach them, and draw them
into relationship with you.
Our lives are incomplete without
you, Lord. Send your grace to
those who are struggling.

And David danced before the Lord
with all his might.

2 Samuel 6:14

Have you ever been overwhelmed with
gratitude toward God? Ever started singing a
favorite hymn or worship song just because
you wanted to let God know how much you
love him? That's the work of God's Spirit in
us, filling us with praise, thanks, and love.
These are precious offerings held in God's
treasury of remembrance, just as we hold
our own children's love gifts close to our
hearts. Perhaps there is a love gift you would
care to offer your heavenly Father even now
as you consider his goodness.

> While the earth remaineth,
> seedtime and harvest, and cold
> and heat, and summer and winter,
> and day and night shall not cease.
>
> Genesis 8:22

Thank you, Lord, at the harvest time. Thank you for the plants that grow to give us food and thank you for the people who grow them. Earth's bounty is a miracle! As I enjoy fresh food, may I always be grateful for what I eat and the nutrition it provides.

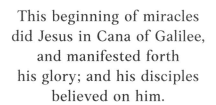

This beginning of miracles
did Jesus in Cana of Galilee,
and manifested forth
his glory; and his disciples
believed on him.

John 2:11

Today I will think about
the miracles in my life. I am
thankful that God gives me
these special gifts. Miracles
remind me that God is always
in my life. Thank you, Lord,
for showing me your power
and surprising me with these
moments of grace. Help me
see your hand at work and
trust that your way is
the best.

Dost thou know the balancings
of the clouds, the wondrous
works of him which is perfect
in knowledge?

Job 37:16

How beautiful is the work of your
hands, Lord! I am grateful for the
world of nature. How wonderful
it is to see the plants and animals
you have created. How awesome
is your power on the shape of
the earth! Thank you, Lord,
for making the landscape and
creating so much beauty in the
natural world.

> Hear instruction, and be wise,
> and refuse it not.
>
> Proverbs 8:33

Thank you for people who share their wisdom. Sometimes I may think I know everything, trusting in my own intelligence, but it is good to realize that there are many people who are smarter than me. What a gift to receive their guidance in my life! Help me to have a listening ear and always be grateful for those who want to help me.

The Lord is the portion of mine
inheritance and of my cup:
thou maintainest my lot.
The lines are fallen unto me
in pleasant places; yea,
I have a goodly heritage.

Psalm 16:5–6

Today I thank you for my
parents and grandparents, and
all those people who taught me
faith through their example. They
modeled prayer and forgiveness
and trust in you. I like to think I
would have found my way to you,
Lord, even without those gifts—
or perhaps it's more that you
would have found your way to
me! But being brought up around
faith-filled people made it easier
when I had questions or problems
or doubts. I want to pass on that
faith to my children, and any
friends or family members who
look up to me.

One Lord, one faith, one baptism,
One God and Father of all,
who is above all, and through all,
and in you all.

Ephesians 4:5–6

Father God, I thank you for your guiding love for me, the love of a father who wants what's best for his child. I can trust in your goodness, and your love is the foundation of my life. I thank you for all the gifts you have given me, but most of all, the gift of your love and abiding presence.

> Let my prayer be set forth before thee as incense; and the lifting up of my hands as the evening sacrifice.
>
> Psalm 141:2

In the evening and morning and noonday we praise thee, we thank thee, and pray thee, Master of all, to direct our prayers as incense before thee. Let not our hearts turn away to words or thoughts of wickedness, but keep us from all things that might hurt us; for to thee, O Lord, our eyes look up, and our hope is in thee: confound us not, O our God; for the sake of Jesus Christ our Lord.

3rd-century Christian prayer

I cried to you,
and you did save.
Your word of grace
new courage gave.
The kings of earth
shall thank you, Lord,
for they have heard
your wondrous word.
Yea, they shall come
with songs of praise,
for great and glorious
are your ways,
for great and glorious
are your ways.

"With Grateful Heart
My Thanks I Bring"

My soul, now praise your Maker!
Let all within me bless his name
who makes you full partaker
of mercies more than you dare claim.
Forget him not whose meekness
still bears with all your sin,
who heals your ev'ry weakness,
renews your life within;
whose grace and care are endless
and saved you through the past;
who leaves no suff'rer friendless
but rights the wronged at last.

Johann Poliander, trans.
Catherine Winkworth

362

And God made two great lights;
the greater light to rule the day,
and the lesser light to rule the night:
he made the stars also.

Genesis 1:16

Thank you for astronomical wonders.
Solar and lunar eclipses, harvest moons,
times when a planet is very clearly visible,
meteor showers—they all provoke wonder
in your creation. Staring up at the sky,
I am aware of how small I am, and how
grand your works. And even when I am
alone, I know others are looking up at the
same sky and experiencing that same awe.

For thou art my hope,
O Lord God:
thou art my trust
from my youth.

Psalm 71:5

My Father,
for another night
of quiet sleep and rest,
for all the joys
of morning light,
thy holy name
be blest. Amen.

Traditional prayer

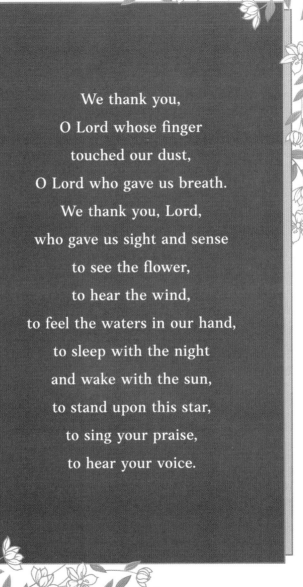

We thank you,
O Lord whose finger
touched our dust,
O Lord who gave us breath.
We thank you, Lord,
who gave us sight and sense
to see the flower,
to hear the wind,
to feel the waters in our hand,
to sleep with the night
and wake with the sun,
to stand upon this star,
to sing your praise,
to hear your voice.

Heal me, O Lord, and I shall
be healed; save me, and I shall
be saved: for thou art my praise.

Jeremiah 17:14

Praise the Lord, for he has seen the affliction
and heard the groans of his people—both
his children who were slaves in Egypt and
we who were in bondage to physical pain.
Indeed, he has come to me in my darkest
moment and rescued me from my misery. He
is a compassionate and wonderful God, who
loves his children and watches over each one
of us. We trust in his mercy.

But ye are a chosen generation,
a royal priesthood, an holy nation,
a peculiar people; that ye should shew
forth the praises of him
who hath called you out of darkness
into his marvellous light.

1 Peter 2:9

Lord, today I pray I will stop taking all
your miraculous works for granted.
Whether I praise you through
song, words, or actions, I want
to praise you not only for what
you are doing, but also for all
you have done in the past.
Help me see the holiness of the
ordinary in each day.

Hear, O ye kings; give ear,
O ye princes; I, even I, will sing
unto the Lord; I will sing praise
to the Lord God of Israel.

Judges 5:3

Lord, just when I was
thinking I was too pooped to
get through the day, I heard
a praise song on the radio.
It reminded me of the
unending supply of energy
and strength that is ours
through faith in you! Thanks
for getting me through the day
today, Lord. I would be so lost
without you.

And I will make them and the places
round about my hill a blessing;
and I will cause the shower
to come down in his season;
there shall be showers of blessing.

Ezekiel 34:26

Dear God,

It's been difficult lately. One challenge after
another, one obstacle after the next. But I
trust everything is for my greatest growth
and to teach me valuable lessons, and for that
I come to you today to give thanks and praise.
I may get angry and frustrated when life gets
derailed, but I know in my heart you are
never giving me more than I can handle,
and that there is a blessing on the other side
of each lesson you provide me with. Those
blessings are what keep me going, even on
the most troubling of days. Thank you for
caring about me enough to push me and
motivate me to grow, to become a stronger,
better person through my trials and
tribulations. I truly am blessed. Amen.

Let the heaven and earth praise him,
the seas, and every thing
that moveth therein.

Psalm 69:34

Today I thank you for the beautiful, often mysterious creatures of the seas and oceans. From the intricate ecosystems of tide pools to the massive forms of blue whales, you created it all! I wonder if the joy of dolphins as they flip and spin and play is their way of singing praise to you? I praise you for the marvels of our world!

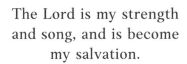

The Lord is my strength
and song, and is become
my salvation.

Psalm 118:14

It's a good day to sing. Not
some country or pop tune.
Sing praise to God, who is
your strength and salvation.
"Amazing Grace." That will
do. How about "Jesus Loves
Me," or some other song you
learned in Sunday school?
Sing it out loud. Embarrass
yourself. Ours is a God
worthy to be praised. And
you don't have to wait until
Sunday morning. He has
put a song in your heart.
Sing it.

Give unto the Lord,
ye kindreds of the people,
give unto the Lord glory
and strength. Give unto the Lord
the glory due unto his name:
bring an offering, and come
before him: worship the Lord
in the beauty of holiness.

1 Chronicles 16:28–29

The greatest offering we can bring to God is praise. Our worship is about this, praise for his glory, strength, name, and beauty. Pause to reflect on the greatness of God today. Then say it out loud: Lord, you are worthy of my praise. Make this your offering today: lips that praise him and a heart that treasures him, awed by his holiness and content with his love. Add more to the list and worship God.

> And they departed, and went through
> the towns, preaching the gospel,
> and healing every where.
>
> Luke 9:6

Dear Lord, thank you for healing my heart and bringing joy and meaning back into my life. Thank you for the people who truly care for me. Help me be a soothing and joyful presence in their lives as well. Amen.

And let the peace of God rule
in your hearts, to the which
also ye are called in one body;
and be ye thankful.

Colossians 3:15

Gratitude may be the most highly
underestimated virtue. We think of love,
hope, faith, and the power of prayer and
forgiveness. But how often do we stop each
day and give thanks for all the blessings in
our lives? Are we too focused on what we
lack, what we don't have, don't want, don't
need? By opening the heart and mind to
focus on gratitude, we unleash a treasure
of unceasing good that's just waiting to
overflow into our lives. A grateful person
knows that by giving thanks, they're given
even more to be thankful for.

But mine eyes are unto thee,
O God the Lord:
in thee is my trust;
leave not my soul destitute.

Psalm 141:8

Father, this morning I woke up, and the gift of life was still within me. What a privilege! I don't want to lose wonder of it for even one day. So help me to live with purpose and joy, not waiting for what today might bring me, but rather looking for opportunities to be and do all that you've created me for. And, most of all, thank you for being with me in each moment, showing me the way of abundant living.

Lord in heaven,
please help me
to see the angels
that I know you have
placed in my presence.
Help me to slow down
and know that
I am always
divinely protected
and guided.
And guide me toward
your angels
to spread your word,
do your work,
be kind, and love.
Thank you, Lord, for
your help this day.

And he said unto them, Come ye yourselves apart into a desert place, and rest a while.

Mark 6:31

Today I am tired, Lord. There seem to be too many things on my to-do list and too few hours in the day. And still, I know what a blessing it is to have work to do and to live a purpose-filled life. Thank you for tasks large and small that give meaning to our days, Lord. May we always do each one as if we were doing it only for you. And may we never assume we can do anything without your direction and energy.

Jesus answered and said unto him,
Verily, verily, I say unto thee,
Except a man be born again,
he cannot see the kingdom of God.

John 3:3

Spiritual birth is amazing, Father! It's a miracle no less exciting than the birth of a baby. Your Word says that it causes even the angels in heaven to rejoice. Thank you for my own spiritual birth. It's the reason I'm praying right now and enjoying this fellowship with you. It's so good to be your child. Today I'll just bask in that reality.

And the Lord was gracious unto them, and had compassion on them.

2 Kings 13:23

Lord, what compassion you showered on your people when you grouped us into families! Thank you, Lord, for the homes we are privileged to enjoy. We are thankful for these sanctuaries for our children and grandchildren. May our homes and our families honor you, Lord, in all we say and do within them. Dwell with us, Lord. You are always welcome.

Apply thine heart
unto instruction,
and thine ears to the words
of knowledge.

Proverbs 23:12

Lord, in your infinite wisdom you knew we would need instruction for life, and so you placed in your Word the guidelines for living a productive life that brings you glory. Your Word nurtures us body and soul and keeps our minds focused on loving, trusting, and obeying you. Thank you, Lord, for not leaving us here without a guidebook. We'd be lost without your Word.

> Therefore it is no great thing
> if his ministers also be transformed
> as the ministers of righteousness;
> whose end shall be
> according to their works.
>
> 2 Corinthians 11:15

Here we are again, Lord. Another time when I feel like I've made a complete mess of this life you've given me. I place myself in your hands, trusting in your wisdom. If you need to totally reshape me to turn me into someone more useful, so be it! Thank you for not abandoning me, your humble creation. Make me over in your design.

Glory and honour are in
his presence; strength
and gladness are in his place.

1 Chronicles 16:27

Lord, how blessed we are
to be able to see you
all around us and to
sense your presence within
us. Even though we can't
see you in the same way
we might see a friend or a
neighbor, we trust in your
presence. We see you in your
Word and in all that is good
and true in the world around
us. Thank you, Lord, for making
yourself so available to us.

Now the God of hope fill you
with all joy and peace in believing,
that ye may abound in hope,
through the power of the Holy Ghost.

Romans 15:13

Thank you, Father, for your Holy Spirit,
who guides me through each day. May I
willingly follow his lead, no matter when
or where. Help me to trust steadily and
obey quickly when he directs me to
serve or forgive others. May I always be
thankful and rejoice in the blessings he
points out to me along the way.

For the Lamb which is in
the midst of the throne
shall feed them, and shall lead
them unto living fountains
of waters: and God shall wipe
away all tears from their eyes.

Revelation 7:17

The older I get, the more aware
I am of the seasons of life,
Lord. I know that when we
draw our energy and resources
from your living Word, we
truly can be compared to the
trees that thrive near streams
of water. The fruit of a young
life lived for you may look a bit
different than the fruit visible
in the lives of older folks, but
it all brings you glory. Thank
you, Lord, for supplying your
living water through all the
seasons of our lives. Without it,
we could bear no worthy fruit
at all.